‹O› Meltwater

CHAMPIONS
CHESS TOUR
2021

T0094770

REGULAR	MAJOR	REGULAR
EUROPEAN OPEN	**MAGNUS CARLSEN INVITATIONAL**	**RAPID CHALLENGE**
Feb 6 - Feb 14	Mar 13 - Mar 21	Apr 24 - May 2
MAJOR	REGULAR	REGULAR
CHESSABLE MASTERS	**INDIAN OPEN**	**LEGENDS OF CHESS**
May 23- May 31	Jun 26 - Jul 4	Jul 31 - Aug 8

REGULAR	
US OPEN	**FINAL**
Aug 28 - Sep 5	Sep 25 - Oct 3

Learn more at: championschesstour.com

Proudly supported by

 AIRTHINGS   ◯ Opera   **Julius Bär**

chessable   **chess24**   **⋈ PLAY MAGNUS**
THE MAGNUS CARLSEN COMPANY

Using the New In Chess app is easy!

- get early access to every issue
- replay all games in the Gameviewer

Sign in with your username and password to access the digital issue.

Read the article, optimized for your screen size.

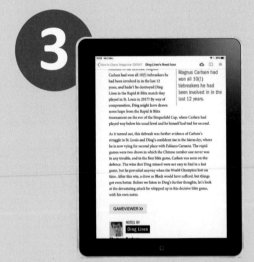

Click on the Gameviewer button to get to the built-in chess board.

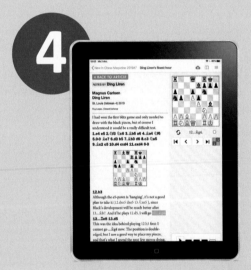

Replay the game, including an option to analyze with Stockfish.

The only chess magazine that moves

www.newinchess.com/chess-apps – for tablet, phone and PC

2021#1

NEW IN CHESS

Contents

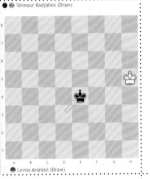

TEIMOUR RADJABOV 1.5

LEVON ARONIAN 0.5

'Sadly, I haven't yet found out how to use Slav theory in everyday life'

CONTRIBUTORS TO THIS ISSUE

Simen Agdestein, Vladimir Barsky, Maxim Dlugy, Daniil Dubov, Anish Giri, John Henderson, Sergey Karjakin, Larry Kaufman, Ian Nepomniachtchi, Maxim Notkin, Judit Polgar, Teimour Radjabov, Oleg Romanishin, Matthew Sadler, Han Schut, David Smerdon, Jan Timman, Thomas Willemze, Jennifer Yu

Ladies Playing Chess

Street art has been booming in Kaunas, Lithuania, for quite some time now. What kicked off as (most often) an illegal pastime, a form of protest and a way of expression, has turned into a colourful flow of murals appreciated by both the society and the municipality.

The boom can be traced to the first edition of the now annual Nykoka Street Art Festival in 2014. But the real explosion in street art came at the beginning of 2017 when Kaunas was chosen to be one of the European Culture Capitals in 2022. This started a city-wide programme of stunning murals that sprang up all over the city, with areas being designated as 'halls of fame' to the arts, music, philosophy and literature.

Transforming street art and finding new canvases for it aren't unusual, too – and chess didn't miss out. One stunning mural covers the wall of the Kaunas University of Technology, and shows a mix of chess and art, with two famous renaissance art world characters turned contemporary, wearing headphones across the chessboard from each other.

Ladies playing Chess' was painted by Lithuanian street artist Linas Kaziulionis (founder of the creative studio K ART 7), who specializes in combining classical icons with street art to bring them closer to a younger audience. The mural depicts modernized fragments of Leonardo da Vinci's famous paintings *Lady with an Ermine* (from the Czartorytski Collection in Krakow) and *La Belle Ferronnière* (or *Portrait of a Woman of the Court of Milan*, from the Louvre in Paris).

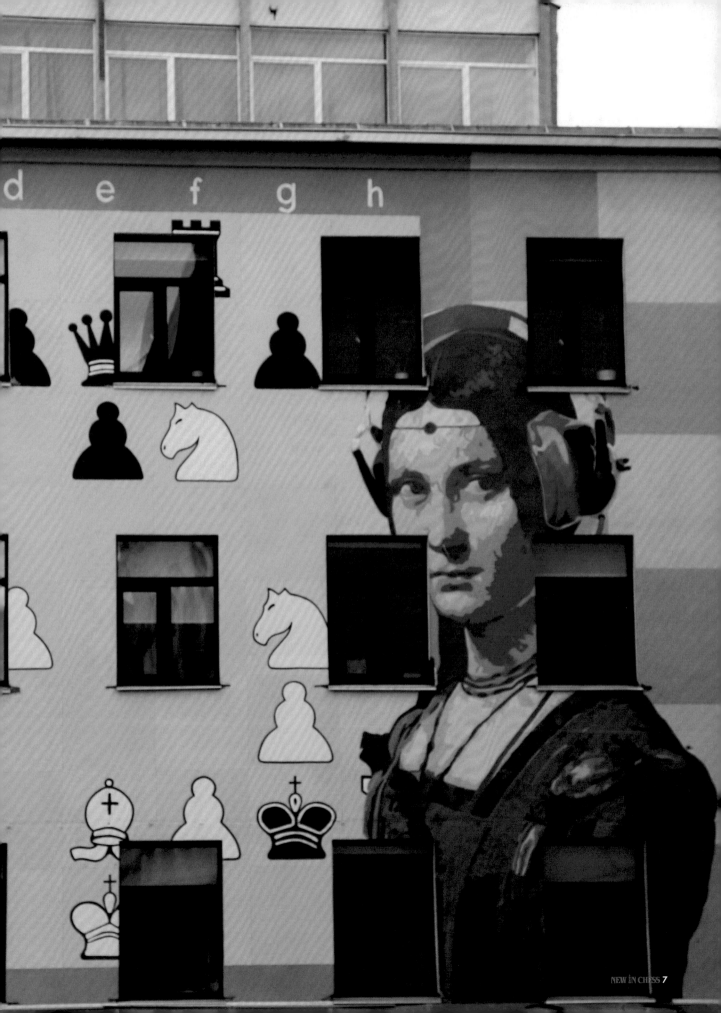

Live like Beth

There's no end to the hype over Netflix's *The Queen's Gambit*. Everyone is getting in on the act, the latest coming in Beth Harmon's own (and author Walter Tevis') hometown of Lexington, Kentucky. The latest edition of *Tatler*, the high society life-

The Harmon Room: a room with a view of the ceiling.

style magazine, featured a top hotel with its own *Queen's Gambit*-inspired suite based on the miniseries.

Called 'The Harmon Room' in 21c Museum Hotels, it comes with a 1960s décor, allowing you to relive all your *Queen's Gambit* fantasies... well, some of them at least. The limited-time hotel room includes an in-room chess set and board as well as a larger-than-life chessboard and pieces glued to the ceiling over the bed, so you can experience one of Beth's drug-induced visions of her own chess games.

The room is also filled with period furniture while the walls are covered in a custom chess-themed wallpaper called 'The Knight's Gambit' which was exclusively created by Alex K Mason of Ferrick Mason Inc. The *Chess Review* magazine you see in the series also makes an appearance here, including some of Beth's chess books.

Hooray for Bollywood

We've been captivated by one fictional chess heroine on the small screen, and now comes the real deal on the big screen. News has emerged from India that a biopic

on the life and times of Vishy Anand is in the works with a film deal agreed and penned by the five-time ex-World Champion.

The movie, whose cast and shooting schedule hasn't been finalized, will be directed by leading Bollywood director Anand L. Rai of *Tanu Weds Manu* fame. Anand is already looking forward to going through the script with his wife Aruna. 'I will be very respectful and open because they are the experts,' Anand told *The Indian Express*. 'I can never come close to their skill in using a camera. I expect to have 25 per cent of the say in the movie but not more than that.'

Anand says he has kept an open mind about the project and isn't sure who will play him. He's also known to be fiercely protective of his privacy but insists that the movie will open a window into his personal life and

Let's speculate who will play the leading role in the Vishy Anand biopic!

further debunk the notion that 'chess players are from an alien planet'.

The yet-untitled biopic, he adds, should look to simplify chess for the masses and not dumb it down.

Show me the money

In previous years, writing about the online gaming high-earners was a simple task, as the usual suspects claimed all the prize winnings. But not in 2020, it seems. According to a mid-December report from *The Esports Observer*, the Covid-19 pandemic resulted in the

cancellation of several major international hybrid esports competitions (such as the Dota 2's The International), a big fall in annual earnings,

Magnus Carlsen: 2020 esports earner top-dog.

and chess now muscling in on the prize-money rankings for the first time.

Through 2020, Magnus Carlsen became the esports earner top-dog thanks in large to the creation of his own pandemic-inspired signature chess tour. The World Champion dominated the online prize-winning rankings for the year, raking in a cool $499,420. Behind him, the Call of Duty League's Dallas Empire team, led by James 'Clayster' Eubanks, took the next five spots, with each picking up in excess of $300K.

And there's a second chess Grandmaster in the Top 10, as Hikaru Nakamura single-handedly raised the online profile of chess. Coupled with his strong placings in the Magnus Carlsen Chess Tour, the US speed maven finds himself in 8th place with $289,810.

Chess! What is it good for?

From ancient India to the computer age, the military has used chess as both a metaphor and even as a role playing game for warfare. The latest to enlist is the School of Infantry-West at Camp Pendleton, California, who have added the teaching of chess to their military school curriculum.

The US Marine Corps are using

chess to help revolutionize their infantry training, looking to use brain and brawn to help bolster high-end threats on the battlefield. Chess is being used as part of a 14-week basic training that starts in late January in the new Infantry Marine Course (IMC).

The idea of including chess came when SOI-West's IT Battalion officials took a deep dive into infantry training. They wanted to find how the training should develop Marines who have a broad array of combat skills they'll need in future battlefields likely spread out and far from higher-level commanders.

Chess was among the unconventional and unorthodox ideas they

No idle pastime. These Marines are building more cognitive capability!

came up with to build more cognitive capability. Training isn't just about telling Marines to 'think more' but rather to engage them in ways where they can exercise their creativity with a war-fighting mindset.

It's hoped that chess will allow 'the Marines to contextually understand where he or she exists in battlespace,' says Chief Warrant Officer Amatangelo Pasciuti, one of the senior course instructors. By introducing it early in the training, the aim is to teach them to think and become conditioned to make decisions.

We understand that America's Foundation for Chess, the Washington State-based group who specialize in putting chess in the class-

room, have already reached out to help develop the IMC's chess course.

Dinner and a rematch

We all have our own special way to spend the last night of the year. As the embers of the final hours were dying out, the members of the versatile US rock band Phish organized a special New Year's Eve-edition of their quarantine livestream video series for a charity rematch of their band vs audience chess rivalry from 25 years ago.

Billed as *Dinner and a Rematch*, the long-awaited grudge match – hosted on Chess.com – came with a stream of their infamous 1995 New Year's Eve concert at Madison Square Garden shown in its entirety. That night the storied chess match came to a close, after the band had played their audience during an intensive US tour one move per gig, using a giant demo board on the stage.

In the end, despite a valiant showing from the fans who registered to play, band members Trey Anastasio, Jon Fishman, Mike Gordon, and Page McConnell prevailed – but not before the onslaught of 20,000+ Phish fans temporarily crashed Chess.com's site! The minor technical snafu was quickly resolved, and a fun-filled New Year's Eve chess night with Phish was had by all, with the

In Madison Square Garden or at home, the members of Phish love chess.

beneficiary being their own charitable organization The WaterWheel Foundation.

Jazzin' up chess

What do you do with a dysfunctional vintage chess computer? One novel solution comes from computer scientist and audio-visual artist Leo Neumann, who, after discussing with a musician

From chess to jazz, just a small step for mankind.

friend about turning old objects into musical instruments, wondered if he could do likewise with his obsolete late 1970s Novag Chess Champion MK 1.

The clicky keyboard was the only thing that still functioned on it, and after realizing the striking similarities between chess notation and chord notation, he had his 'lightbulb moment' by transforming it into a prototype melody generator – a jazz chord game where to score points, you jam with the computer.

Neumann, of tonlichtstudio in Lübeck, Germany, a company that makes interactive music and light machines, says that the user and the computer take turns inputting jazz chords, ultimately making up the melody. 'For example,' he explained on its launch, 'a pawn moves from the square e7 to e6. In jazz, this would mean that the E major chord is progressing. This allowed me to reuse the keyboard with only minor changes.'

In keeping with the original design and name of his old Novag chess computer, Neumann decided to find suitable outside parts that resembled its retro style for the launch of his 'Jazz Champion MK 1'. ∎

White players will thoroughly dislike this!

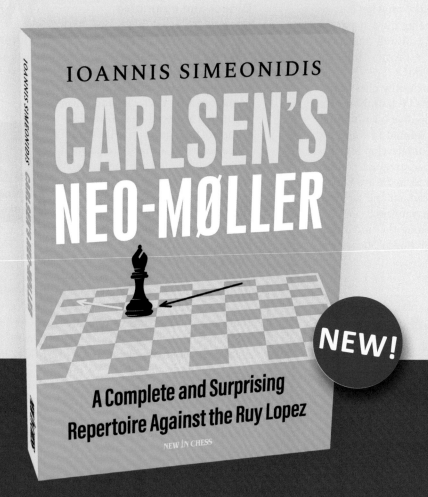

Black players allowing the Ruy Lopez main lines are usually condemned to passivity. World Champion Magnus Carlsen doesn't like that. That's why he revolutionized the old Møller Attack. As yet largely disregarded and unexplored by the majority of players, Carlsen's new approach allows Black to break free early and start giving White a hard time.

FM Ioannis Simeonidis is the first to investigate this system, cover it in detail, and make it easy to grasp for club players. He has called it the Neo-Møller. Simeonidis has made lots of exciting discoveries, presents many new ideas and shows that it is a reliable and playable system.

Since the Neo-Møller is a very early deviation from the main lines, it's easy for Black to actually get it on the board and take opponents out of their comfort zone. Simeonidis has created a compact, accessible and inspirational book. One thing looks certain: White players of the Ruy Lopez are going to thoroughly dislike the Neo-Møller!

paperback | 160 pages | €22.95 | available at your local (chess)bookseller or at newinchess.com | a NEW IN CHESS publicatio

Two typos

In New In Chess 2020/8, in Thomas Willemze's article, a rook was left *en prise* but not taken.

Willemze analyses the move 14... f5 giving a variation 15.exf5 ♗xf5 16.♗d3 and a sub-note of 16...♘d7 saying that then 17.♗xf5 ♖xf5 18.♕c2! is good for White.

Of course, 18.♖xf5, winning a whole rook, is better for White! Unless, of course, it was meant to be 16...♕d7 (instead of 16...♘d7), and then it all makes sense.

Earlier in the day I'd been looking at John Donaldson's *Bobby Fischer and His World* and a similar thought struck me. On pages 53-54 there is a game Fischer-Spector, New York 1956. Donaldson analyses up to **13...♘e5?**

when he says that 'After the text Fischer wins in convincing fashion' and gives no more notes. After:
14.♗e2 h5 15.h4 ♘c4 16.♖d4 ♘a5 17.♘xa5 ♕xa5 18.♖a4 ♕b6 19.♖b4 ♕a5 20.♗e3 ♘d7 the move 21.♖d4 is given, which after 21...♕e5 22.♗f4 leaves the d4-rook hanging. Of course, it would all make

sense if Bobby had played **21.♖a4** hitting his opponent's queen.

So two rook blunders which were typos. An unusual haul for a day!

By the way, I am loving Donaldson's book on Fischer, and New In Chess, and I have great respect for Thomas Willemze as an author as I have his book *The Chess Toolbox*, which I think is excellent.

Carl Gorka
Drouin, Australia

Editorial postscript:
Two typos that cannot be blamed on the original texts! Thomas Willemze did write 16...♕d7, which for some inexplicable reason was changed into 16...♘d7. And John Donaldson informs us that Bobby Fischer indeed wrote 21.♖a4 on his scoresheet.

Write to us
New In Chess, P.O. Box 1093
1810 KB Alkmaar, The Netherlands
or e-mail: editors@newinchess.com
Letters may be edited or abridged

Candidates stars

Now that FIDE has announced the postponement of the Candidates' conclusion until March 2021, we might console ourselves by looking back at the results of past editions. The Candidates tournament is the gate towards the chess summit, and taking part in just one of them is the privilege of a few chosen ones. Revisiting its history, that dates back to Budapest 1950, gives us a fascinating perspective of those players that dominated the chess scene, including chess greats that never reached the highest title.

One might then wonder who has been the greatest performer. The following data might be of interest to the reader (note: not included are FIDE events during the schism from 1993 until 2006).

In terms of the number of participations, Viktor Kortchnoi comes out as the absolute king, having competed in ten(!) Candidates, closely followed by Tigran

Petrosian (who was World Champion for 6 years) and Lajos Portisch, both with 8 participations.

In terms of success, Anatoly Karpov seems to be on top, as he won the Candidates a record three times, whereas Kortchnoi managed to win it twice (he also twice finished second), a feat equalled only by Smyslov, Spassky and Anand.

Finally, if one considers the Elo performance, Bobby Fischer's magical run of 18½ points out of 21 games in his 1971 matches against Mark Taimanov, Bent Larsen and Tigran Petrosian clearly stands out.

But since opinions are free, I prefer to choose Paul Keres, who, while never becoming World Champion, managed to finish second in four consecutive Candidates and won the very strong pre-war tournaments at Semmering 1937 and AVRO 1938, both of which were referred to as 'Candidates' though not officially recognized as such by FIDE. Any suggestions?

Fernando Luis
Zaragoza, Spain

COLOPHON

PUBLISHER: Allard Hoogland
EDITOR-IN-CHIEF:
Dirk Jan ten Geuzendam
HONORARY EDITOR: Jan Timman
CONTRIBUTING EDITOR: Anish Giri
EDITORS: Peter Boel, René Olthof
PRODUCTION: Joop de Groot
TRANSLATORS: Ken Neat, Piet Verhagen
SALES AND ADVERTISING: Remmelt Otten

PHOTOS AND ILLUSTRATIONS IN THIS ISSUE:
Vladimir Barsky, Maria Emelianova, Eteri Kublashvili,
Lennart Ootes, Koen Suyk, Berend Vonk

COVER PICTURE: New In Chess

© No part of this magazine may be reproduced, stored in a retrieval system or transmitted in any form or by any means, recording or otherwise, without the prior permission of the publisher.

NEW IN CHESS
P.O. BOX 1093
1810 KB ALKMAAR
THE NETHERLANDS

PHONE: 00-31-(0)72-51 27 137
SUBSCRIPTIONS: nic@newinchess.com
EDITORS: editors@newinchess.com
ADVERTISING: otten@newinchess.com

WWW.NEWINCHESS.COM

Teimour Radjabov still has the moves

Teimour Radjabov cannot hide his emotions as he wins the Airthings Masters by beating Levon Aronian in the final.

The online Airthings Masters took a very unpredictable course as one favourite after the other fell by the wayside. Carlsen, Nakamura, So – none of them even made it to the last hurdle. The big winner was 33-year-old Teimour Radjabov, who defeated Levon Aronian in the final, cashed $60,000 and qualified for the final of the Meltwater Champions Chess Tour in San Francisco. **SIMEN AGDESTEIN** reports.

After nine strenuous days over Christmas, Teimour Radjabov could no longer contain himself. He raised his fists and cried, tears rolling down his cheeks, as he realized that he had won the Airthings Masters. 'I am completely exhausted', he confirmed. 'Trying to keep the focus and concentration to the very end takes a lot of emotions.'

As the annus horribilis 2020 faded out, the Azeri grandmaster may have seen a new dawn. On the third day of 2021, Radjabov claimed the $60,000 first prize of the total $200,000 prize fund as he beat Levon Aronian in the final. With his win in the second leg of the new Meltwater Champions Chess Tour 2021, Radjabov also secured a place in the final tournament in San Francisco next September, which, if possible, will be an in-person event.

33-year-old Radjabov was once a child prodigy and a potential World Championship contender. Eight years ago, he was ranked fourth in the world, but his road had been bumpy for the past few years. His withdrawal from the Candidates Tournament last year, in connection with the outbreak of Covid-19, attracted worldwide attention. Although history may have proven him right, it doesn't look likely that he will regain his place in the suspended Candidates; but at least this win may have strengthened his case.

Radjabov joins Wesley So, the winner of the Skilling Open, the first leg of the Tour, as a finalist. Altogether there will be nine qualifying tournaments; one every month.

Political overtones

It's been a while since chess competitions had heavy political overtones, such as the 1972 Fischer-Spassky match during the Cold War, and the clashes between Karpov and Soviet dissident Kortchnoi. There was some fear that the final between Radjabov and Aronian might be affected by the military conflict between Azerbaijan and Armenia over the Nagorno-Karabakh region. However, we saw no sign of this. Radjabov and Aronian both appeared perfectly sympathetic and intelligent. NRK, the main Norwegian TV channel, broadcast it all, even the final days after Magnus Carlsen had been eliminated. They also had inside reports from the respective countries showing that no-one tried to use the final match for political purposes. Rather the opposite, you might say. Perhaps

two four-game matches played over two days. In case the two results combined produced a level score, two blitz games were played, and if these didn't produce a winner, an Armageddon would decide the final verdict.

A definite risk of the preliminary round-robin is that the players proceed cautiously, since not losing may be more efficient than taking risks to win. This time, the system certainly led to many draws, since the

Perhaps out of fear that their idol might lose, attention for the final was lowered both in Baku and in Yerevan

out of fear that their idol might lose, attention for the final was lowered both in Baku and in Yerevan.

Again the Airthings Masters started with a preliminary round-robin tournament with 12 players. Of these, eight qualified for the knockout stages, which consisted of

main objective seemed to be to avoid finishing in one of the last four places. In the end, the pack was still very much a pack, with only two points separating the top from the bottom. The four players that failed to qualify were Harikrishna, Grischuk, Giri and Anton.

The 'undisclosed location' from where Magnus Carlsen was playing turned out to be the Seychelles. Fortunately, the World Champion's busy schedule also included chess.

Caucasian final

The knock-out phase saw the sensational elimination of the top favourites. More about them later. Let's first have a look at the finalists, the two Caucasian stars who fought for the title. On the first day of the final, they started off with three interesting draws. For some reason, Aronian seemed to be very keen on taking the lead and winning the first match, because in the fourth game he invested a pawn for the initiative against the ultra-solid Berlin Defence. And even when the computer showed

a clear Black advantage, he declined Radjabov's suggestion of a draw by repetition.

Levon Aronian
Teimour Radjabov
Airthings Masters 2020 (final 1.4)
Ruy Lopez, Berlin Defence

1.e4 e5 2.♘f3 ♘c6 3.♗b5 ♘f6 4.0-0 ♘xe4 5.d4 ♘d6 6.♗xc6 dxc6 7.dxe5 ♘f5 8.♕xd8+ ♔xd8 9.h3 ♗d7 10.♖d1 ♔c8 One of the commentators on Chess24, Tania Sachdev, was very doubtful about the combination 'Berlin' and 'sharp',

but that's exactly what we soon got.
11.g4 ♘e7 12.♘g5 ♗e8 13.f4

13...c5!? This has only been played

Tania Sachdev, was very doubtful about the combination 'Berlin' and 'sharp', but that's exactly what we soon got

twice. 13...h6 and 13...h5 are the most heavily discussed lines. **14.♘c3 b6**

15.f5!? Now the game takes a unique course. Both Sutovsky-Harikrishna, Ningbo 2011 (0-1), and Dominguez-Melkumyan, Baku 2015 (1-0), saw 15.♔f2. **15...♘c6 16.♗f4 ♘d4**

17.♔f2 There are many ways to play this line, so it's hard to imagine that Aronian had prepared this highly risky pawn sacrifice in exactly this position; but Peter Leko said he recognized the idea. The computer suggests a slight White advantage after 17.e6. **17...h6 18.♘f3 ♘xc2 19.♖ac1 ♘b4 20.a3 ♘c6 21.♘d5 ♘e7 22.♘e3 ♘c6**

23.f6?! Very ambitious. In hindsight, offering repetition with 23.♘d5 seems wiser. **23...♗d7 24.b4** Again, 24.♘d5, now with the idea 24...g5 25.♘xc7!?, seems better.

24...g5! 25.♗g3 ♗e6 Radjabov has established the perfect set-up. **26.♖d3 ♔b7 27.♖dc3 ♖d8 28.♘f5**

Airthings Masters 2020 (preliminaries)

				TPR
1 Carlsen	NOR	2862	6½	2814
2 So	USA	2770	6½	2822
3 Nakamura	USA	2736	6½	2825
4 Nepomniachtchi	RUS	2784	6	2785
5 Radjabov	AZE	2765	6	2787
6 Aronian	ARM	2781	5½	2759
7 Vachier-Lagrave	FRA	2784	5	2733
8 Dubov	RUS	2702	5	2740
9 Harikrishna	IND	2732	5	2738
10 Grischuk	RUS	2777	5	2734
11 Giri	NED	2764	4½	2699
12 Anton Guijarro	ESP	2675	4½	2707

28...a5! Aronian is without counter-play and Radjabov easily activates his pieces. **29.b5 ♞a7 30.a4 c6 31.bxc6+ ♞xc6 32.♔e2 ♞b4 33.♖d1 ♖xd1 34.♔xd1 ♞d5 35.♖a3**

35...c4 The dark-squared bishop finally gets out, and then it's all over. **36.♞d6+ ♝xd6 37.exd6 ♖d8 38.♝e5 ♞b4 39.♝g3 ♞d3 40.♞d4 ♝d7 41.♔d2 ♖e8 42.♞c2 ♞c5 43.♖e3 ♞e4+ 44.♔c1 ♞xg3 45.♖xg3 ♖e6 46.♖c3 ♖xf6 47.♖xc4 ♖xd6 48.♔b2 ♖d3** White resigned.

Aronian continued to take extreme risks in the first game of the second day. Again he ended up in trouble, but this time he got away with a draw. Then Radjabov won the next game relatively smoothly and closed the deal in the third game with an easy draw.

When we asked the winner to comment on one of his wins, Teimour Radjabov chose the following wild skirmish from the semi-finals, against Daniil Dubov.

NOTES BY
Teimour Radjabov

Daniil Dubov
Teimour Radjabov
Airthings Masters 2020 (sf 1.4)
Sicilian Defence, Sveshnikov Variation

This was an important game, played on New Year's Eve, the last one before January 1, 2021. I needed a draw to secure victory in the first set of the semi-finals. But making a draw against Daniil is harder than beating him or losing to him. ☺
1.e4 c5 2.♞f3 ♞c6 3.d4 cxd4 4.♞xd4 e5

The Kalashnikov, my weapon as Black for many years of my career. This time it transposed to the Sveshnikov. It sometimes does, but there are many subtleties.
5.♞b5 d6 6.♞1c3 a6 7.♞a3 b5 8.♞d5 ♞f6
Now White has different ways to play. One is 9.c4, another is 9.♞xf6+ followed by c4. The positions are complicated, with chances for both sides.
9.♝g5
We are back in the ♞d5 line of the Sveshnikov. I did not remember my notes and did not expect it, so please do not repeat my opening play in this game. ☺
9...♝e7 10.♝xf6 ♝xf6 11.c3 ♝g5 12.♞c2 ♖b8 13.h4!?

A very interesting move, that I had not seen in this position before. But it's one of the typical ideas in the Sveshnikov. Now, taking on h4 and

checking what was the idea seemed like a bad approach, but that's actually what Black has to do here!

13...♗h6?

This is pretty bad. After 13...♗xh4 14.g3 ♗g5 15.f4 exf4 16.gxf4 ♗h4+ 17.♔d2 Black cannot castle (because of ♕h5!), but it seems there is a solution here: 17...♔f8!, planning ...g6 and ...♔g7 – Black escapes any danger and is a pawn up in a complicated middlegame battle, where he is not worse at all.

14.♗e2? White could exploit my mistake with 14.a4!, when castling is perhaps the best way for Black to go, but for everyone who understands the Sveshnikov it is terrible to see the weakness on b5, that will be a long-term headache: 14...bxa4 15.♘cb4 ♘xb4 16.♘xb4 ♗d7 and now the problem is that after 17.♕xd6 Black does not have ...♗e7, as the bishop is on h6, which changes the evaluation of the position totally. White is winning.

14...0-0 15.♗g4 Daniil goes for a practical approach. The bishop is planning to get to f5 and provoke ...g6, or otherwise White will play ♕h5.

15...♗e6 The natural move, but maybe 15...♗b7!? was easier. I was afraid to leave the king's flank this way. But Black can play ...♘e7 anytime soon and just parry all of the attacks by White, and ...♘a5 may also be an option. After 16.♗f5, 16...g6 followed by ...♔g7 and ...f5 is perfect for Black.

16.♔f1?!

He wants to go g3/♔g2, but it seems too slow. The immediate 16.g3 followed by ♘de3 would make more

sense. But we should not forget that Daniil needed to win.

16...♕d7?! Better was 16...a5, threatening ...b4, but also taking the b4-square under control: 17.a3 ♘e7 and ♘b4 is never possible.

17.♗f5 A nice trick, if Black takes...

17...♔h8 Sidestepping any ♘e7 checks. After 17...♗xf5? 18.exf5 ♕xf5 19.♘cb4! White wins, as the knight can't be taken due to ♘e7+ picking up the queen.

18.♕h5 A perfect setup in a must-win game: the bishop on h6 is pinned, ♘f6 is in the air, g4 is always possible and the d5-square well controlled. And White's king is safe.

18...♗xf5?

I think tiredness was telling here. Never ever in my life, if fresh and stable, would I go for this concession. I think that Daniil's reply confirms that emotional and physical factors were crucial in our decision-making here, but what is a game without mistakes? Not that exciting usually! Black had two much better ways to continue:

– 18...b4!? 19.cxb4 ♕a7!! 20.a3 ♗xd5 21.exd5 ♘e7 22.♖d1 ♘g8!!.

Brilliant! Love it ☺ ...g6 is threatened and Black has enough counterplay. Or 18...♘e7 19.♘xe7 ♕xe7 20.♖h3 d5 and Black is fine.

19.exf5? We both had missed that 19.♕xf5! gives White a huge advantage! The endgame is bad for Black, due to the bishop on h6 and the pawn on d6, while White's knight on d5 is amazing as well. And after 19...♕e8 20.♖d1 White's play is simple and he is dominating.

19...f6 Now at least the bishop is stable on h6 and immediate threats have been stopped.

20.♖d1

A critical position. Black has to act fast. Once White puts his queen on e4

and the rook comes from h1 to d3, it will be time to resign.

20...a5?!
I thought I could afford this, in order to stop ♘cb4 forever, but it's too slow. Instead, 20...e4! was called for: 21.♖h3 ♖be8, when Black is fully in the game: ...♖e5 is coming and I have enough counterplay.

21.♖h3! Now ♕g4 is next and White will control the light squares. I understood that I had to do something to avoid immediate defeat here.

21...♖be8?
Again, 21...e4! was the way to go.

Teimour Radjabov could not resist pushing the tempting 31...e3?, but 31...♕f2! would quickly have put an end to Daniil Dubov's resistance.

22.♖hd3? I think Daniil had already planned his combination, otherwise exposing the rook to ...e4 is strange. Both 22.♘a3! and 22.♕e2!? would have given White excellent play.

22...e4 23.♘xf6? Going back to h3 was necessary, but admitting that ♖hd3 was a loss of tempo is extremely hard. The sacrifice is objectively bad, but practically venomous.

23...♖xf6 24.♖xd6

24...♖xf5!?
Playing it kind of safe. The e-pawn is good and White's king is vulnerable. After 24...♖xd6!, 25.♖xd6 ♕c8! 26.f6

scared me a lot. I did not see how to proceed and completely missed that after 26...♘e5! 27.f7 I have the important check 27...♕c4+ and I am completely winning!

25.♖xc6 ♖xf2+ 26.♔xf2 ♕xc6 27.♔g1?!
27.♘d4! was a nice resource: 27...♖f8+ (after 27...♕f6+ 28.♔e2!? is a devilish trick: 28...♖f8 (28...♖g8 draws, but looks less natural) 29.♕f5!! and White is winning suddenly!) 28.♔g3 ♕d6+ 29.♔h3 ♕d7+ 30.♕g4 ♕xg4+ 31.♔xg4 ♖f2 and Black keeps the balance.

27...b4

28.cxb4 After 28.♕xa5 I had two options: taking on c3 or playing the

immediate ...e3. Both are good for Black and should lead to a draw.

28...axb4 29.♘xb4 ♕b6+ 30.♔h1 ♖f8
This is much easier to play for Black: ...e3 is coming, h4 is always a target and White's a- and b-pawns are not moving forward. The only thing is not to exchange queens of course.

31.a3? 31.♘c2 ♕xb2 with a draw is not what Daniil wanted, even though it was kind of best.

31...e3?
Nice to have this pawn advanced, but the move misses a quite simple victory: 31...♕f2!, threatening to take on b2 and supporting the e-pawn.

32.♕e5 ♕g6 33.♘d5 ♕c2

Finally hitting on the idea of bringing the queen to help promote the e-pawn!

34.♖g1 34.♖d4 was necessary: 34...♕xb2 35.♖e4 ♕xe5 36.♖xe5 ♖f1+ 37.♔h2 g6 with equality.

34...♕f2! 35.♕e7 e2 36.♘c3

36...♗g5!?

An attractive move and a great one to celebrate the New Year in a good mood!

But 36...g5!! was winning at once! It did not cross my mind at all, as I was thinking about other things, such as 36...♗e3 37.♘xe2 and I thought I was losing, but in fact, after 37...♖g8!!, White has to resign! Unbelievable!

37.♕xg5

As 37.hxg5 ♕h4 is mate.

37...e1♕ 38.♖xe1 ♕xe1+ 39.♔h2 h6 40.♕g3 ♕c1 41.♕d6

41...♖f1

Black wins both after 41...♖g8! and 41...♖c8! 42.♕d7 ♕f4+ 43.♔g1 ♖b8.

42.♕d8+ ♔h7 43.♕d3+ ♔h8

As a draw doesn't bring him anything Daniil keeps looking for a win and overpushes.

44.♘e4 ♖h1+ 45.♔g3 ♕xb2 46.♕d8+ ♔h7 47.♕d3

I could take a draw here, but after he did not take it before and as Black is running no risk, I decided to finish in style! ☺

47...♕e5+ 48.♔g4 ♕e6+ 49.♔f4 ♖xh4+ 50.♔e3 ♖g4 Everything is pinned, Black is winning.

51.♔f3 ♕f5+ 52.♔e3 ♕f4+ 53.♔d4 ♕d6+ White resigned.

I know this game contains many mistakes, which makes these rapid events beautiful and fun to watch and take part in. It also shows the fighting spirit of the players, especially in the knockout stage. I am happy about the result of this tournament and on qualifying to the Grand Final! Looking forward to other great events of this Tour!

■ ■ ■

Tremendous hit

In Norway, the Airthings Masters was hyped as the main sport event this Christmas. The average Norwegian, after hours of chess on prime time TV, not only knows everything about Magnus Carlsen, but has also become familiar with the other chess players. Chess on TV continues to be a tremendous hit – mainly because of Magnus, of course, but after he had been knocked out in the quarter finals by Daniil Dubov, the show went on. At its peak the broadcast of the final attracted 150,000 viewers (which would have been about double if Magnus had been playing).

Also online interest was big. Chess24 had nine(!) channels in different languages (including four different English versions), and there was also an international broadcast on Eurosport.

Magnus's elimination was clearly a setback for the Norwegian audience, and perhaps the organizers, but the road for Play Magnus seems to be paved with roses. When registering on the Norwegian stock exchange some months ago, the company's value was estimated at over 100 million euro, and guess what... in the meantime its value has only gone up.

It was a secret from where exactly Magnus was playing his games, but it surely was a tropical destination. He

The average Norwegian, after hours of chess on prime time TV, not only knows everything about Magnus Carlsen, but has also become familiar with the other chess players

must have felt at ease there, but for some reason he didn't seem to be his normal self. My reasoning is that he is the best, and if he doesn't win, there must be an external reason. Perhaps the ongoing controversy in Norway about his sponsor Unibet played a role. Gambling is a prerogative of the state in Norway, and his affiliation with a betting company has invoked criticism. When it became clear that Magnus was playing with the Unibet logo in the background, NRK reacted and soon blurred the background. But Magnus 'struck back' by declining to give interviews to NRK and he was wearing a shirt with the sponsor's brand shining bright and clear on his chest. His reasoning was that since he was playing abroad, this was legal, while NRK argued that what's shown in Norway is what matters. For a fine-tuned brain like Magnus's and in a sport like ours, where the margins are so small, such frictions can be enough to tip the balance, although it's clear that I'm only speculating.

For Daniil Dubov it was a big moment when he beat the World Champion in the quarter final. His reaction said it all: 'I was much more interested in winning this match than in winning the whole thing!' Magnus has praised Dubov, together with the computer program Leela, for his inspired play during the past year.

The cameras clearly showed the players' spontaneous reactions when the result had become clear, but soon after Magnus generously posted his respect for his opponent: 'On a lighter note, Daniil just wrote to me to cheer me up after beating me and apologize for his celebration on air. Told him I did not see it, and it would upset me more if people stopped celebrating after beating me. Congrats to a most worthy opponent and great dude!'

It all had seemed 'business as usual' when Magnus won a drawish ending in the first game against Dubov. But Dubov fought back and equalized the score, and it wouldn't have been unfair if he'd taken the lead on the first day. With the score tied 2-2 after the first set, Dubov kept up the momentum as he won the first game of the second set.

NOTES BY
Anish Giri

Daniil Dubov
Magnus Carlsen
Airthings 2021 (qf 2.1)
Catalan Opening, Capablanca Variation

1.d4 ♘f6 2.c4 e6 3.♘f3 d5 4.g3 ♗b4+ 5.♘bd2

Daniil Dubov consistently went for this Catalan system in his two mini-matches against Magnus Carlsen. Magnus was changing back and forth, from accepting the c4-pawn with ...dxc4 to the more solid ...0-0, ...b6 setup. In the end, both approaches failed him.

5...0-0 6.♗g2 b6 7.0-0 ♗b7 8.♘e5 There are other moves in this tabiya position. Dubov himself tried 8.b3 against Magnus earlier, for example. And there are some other options as well.

8...a5

9.♕c2!? This may very well have been a slight surprise. White plays a cunning semi-waiting move.

9...a4 A very odd push, but Black does grab some space on the queen-side and practically stops b3.

10.♖d1
Another useful move. White doesn't want to settle for a developing scheme just yet, preferring to stay flexible.

10...♗d6
The bishop gets hit on this square, so finding an improvement here might be a good idea, in case Black wants to go for this position again.

11.cxd5 exd5 12.♘dc4!

A standard idea in this line, exploiting the pin on the d5-pawn.

12...h6 A strong move, since ♘xd6 is not the end of the world, because Black will recapture with the c7-pawn and at least solve the issue of the strong e5-knight.
13.♗f4 White goes for natural development. An excellent idea.
13...♖e8 14.♖ac1 ♘a6

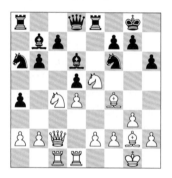

Both sides have finished their development, but while White has a normal set-up aimed at the centre, Black's pieces are a bit odd. Besides the a6-knight, only the a4-pawn is vulnerable.
15.a3 A pretty-looking waiting move; but White should have cashed out on his positional advantage here and finally doubled Black's pawns.
15.♘xd6! cxd6 16.♘c4! would have been strong, hitting the d6-pawn on the way and going for a positional plus based on the bishop pair, Black's pawn weaknesses and his lack of piece coordination.
15...♗f8! Now the bishop hides and escapes the trade.

16.♘e3 Allowing 16...g5, inviting crazy complications.
16...c5!? A sensible idea – playing in the centre and not allowing White to sacrifice a piece.

If Black picks up the gauntlet with 16...g5, there follows 17.♘xf7! ♔xf7 18.♗e5!, with a very dangerous initiative for the sacrificed piece, although objectively Black can fight on with the strong 18...♕d7!, taking control of the g4- and f5-squares. With the black king so weak, most people would still prefer White here. There are plenty interesting ideas on the kingside, connected with h4- or f4-breaks and some knight jumps, e.g. ♘f5.
17.♘f5

Throwing a knight forward and preparing an escape for the f4-bishop if necessary.
17...cxd4
Also possible and quite decent was 17...♘c7!?, maintaining the tension and bringing the knight from the edge of the board towards the centre.
18.♘c6 ♕d7 19.♗h3

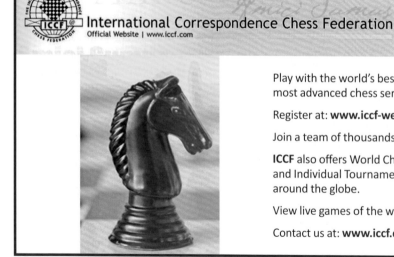

19...♔h8?? Absolutely inexplicable, although Magnus may simply have overlooked the possibility of 20.♘e5. Instead, just capturing twice on c6 would have led to a roughly balanced endgame: 19...♕xc6 (taking with the bishop first is also totally OK, since ♘xh6+ would give Black three pieces for the queen) 20.♕xc6 (after 20.♕b1!? Black can sacrifice his queen in many good ways, e.g. 20...♕e6 21.♘xh6+ gxh6, with ample compensation, because three well-coordinated pieces are worth no less than a queen) 20...♗xc6 21.♖xc6 ♖xe2, and despite the queens having been traded, the position remains highly complicated, although objectively balanced.

20.♘e5!

Magnus Carlsen had barely played the 'absolutely inexplicable' 19...♔h8?? or Peter Leko's expression revealed the commentator's assessment.

Not a hard move to spot, but even the World Champion can have a blind spot once in a while. Black has to give up the exchange.

20...♖xe5 Since 20...♕e6 21.♘xh6 ♕xh3 would fail to 22.♘exf7, mate.

21.♗xe5 ♘e4 22.♗xd4

Magnus is dead lost now, being an exchange down for no compensation, but remarkably enough, he still gets a chance later on.

22...♖c8

23.♕d3

A step in the wrong direction. 23.♕b1! would have been a lot cleaner: 23...♘ac5 24.♗xc5! ♘xc5 25.♗g2. Simple chess. White unpins and will win easily thanks to the extra exchange and complete control of the position.

23...♘ac5 24.♕e3?!

It was better to take on c5 at once to clear up the tension.

24...♔h7 25.♗xc5

White finally captures, since it would have been hard to deal with the potential threat of ...g6 otherwise.

25...♘xc5

26.♕f3?! Simpler was 26.♕f4!, not allowing the ...d4 idea.

26...d4!

Magnus tries to confuse matters as much as possible.

27.♖xd4 ♕e8 Maintaining the

tension, since the tactic wasn't working: 27...♘b3!? (or 27...♘e6!?) is met by the clever 28.♖cd1! ♘xd4 29.♘xd4, and White is still winning.
28.♕e3?! 28.♕g4! was not obvious, but the computer likes it a lot. Black has no follow-up here.
28...♕c6 29.f3 Best was to go back with 29.♕f3, hoping to repeat and then go to g4 with the queen.
29...♖e8! Now Black gets some kind of initiative going.
30.♕f2 g6 31.♘e3 ♕f6!

Suddenly White is uncoordinated in a terrible manner.
32.♘g4 ♕g7 33.♖cd1 h5
White's pieces start getting pushed back.
34.♘e3 ♘b3 35.♘4d3
Now there could be at the very least a highly nasty pin on ♗c5. Magnus goes for a very ambitious pawn capture instead.

35...♕xb2!?
Objectively a fine move, but 35...♗c5! was probably more practical: 36.♗d7 ♖xe3 37.♖xe3 ♕xb2, with a mess, e.g. 38.♗xa4 ♘d2!, and God knows what's going on, but the engine proclaims dynamic equality.

'Dubov-style' became a frequent phrase among the commentators

36.♖d7 ♗c5 Going for the pin.
37.♖xf7+ ♔h6 38.♖dd7

38...♕a1+??
A terrible idea, played probably out of fear of losing on time. Black is only pushing White's king away from the fatal c5-g1 X-ray. Magnus wanted to lure the king to g2 to pin the f3-pawn, but there was not enough time to calculate everything.
38...♕h8!, stopping ♖h7+, would have kept the chaos alive. It is a three-outcome game here, with the computer proclaiming dynamic equality. Next Black captures the e3-knight.
39.♔g2 ♗xe3 40.♖h7+ ♔g5
And now comes the killing blow:

Airthings Masters 2020 (KO finals)

Quarter Finals			
Dubov-Carlsen	2-2	2½-½	
Radjabov-Nepomniachtchi	2-2	2-2	1½-1½
Aronian-Nakamura	2½-1½	2-0	
Vachier-Lagrave-So	3-1	1½-2½	1½-1½

Semi-Finals		
Radjabov-Dubov	3-1	2-0
Aronian-Vachier-Lagrave	3-1	2-1

Final 3rd-4th place		
Dubov-Vachier-Lagrave	2-2	1½-2½

Final		
Radjabov-Aronian	2½-1½	2-1

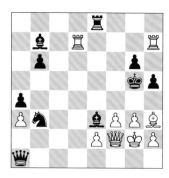

41.♖xb7! Taking the bishop and unpinning the f3-pawn. With f4+ and ♖f7 mate coming, Black is lost.
41...♖f8 42.♕xe3+
Black resigned. A rollercoaster!

■ ■ ■

In the next game, Magnus seemed to regain his composure as he again outplayed his opponent in a seemingly highly drawish endgame. However, this time he didn't bring home the whole point, another clear sign that he wasn't at his best. Game 3 was an absolute thriller. It was also the last game they played, as Dubov's win decided the semi-final in his favour and knocked out the World Champion.

Danill Dubov
Magnus Carlsen
Airthings Masters (qf 2.3)
Catalan Opening, Capablanca Variation
1.d4 ♘f6 2.c4 e6 3.♘f3 d5 4.g3 ♗b4+ 5.♘bd2 This actually occurred in all four games in which Dubov was White.

5...dxc4 In the three previous games, Magnus refrained from taking.
6.♗g2 a5!? The idea is known, but

rare in this particular position. **7.a3
♗xd2+ 8.♗xd2 b5 9.a4** 9.b3, as in
Oparin-Vokhidov, Xingtai 2018, also
gives White long-term compensation.
9...c6 10.♕c2 ♗b7

11.h4! Wow! 'Dubov-style' became a
frequent phrase among the commentators. The man himself modestly said
he wouldn't have had a chance with
slow play against Magnus, so even
in this situation, when a draw would
have secured him two points and at
least a play-off, he sticks to his guns.
11...♘bd7 12.h5 h6 13.♘e5
A slight surprise, since 13.♖h4!?
seemed so 'natural' and perhaps also
more flexible, since the idea g4-g5
might deter Black from castling
kingside.
13...♘d5?! The knight on e5
soon becomes an octopus, and it's
surprising that Magnus lets it live.
14.♖h4 ♘7f6 15.♔f1!?
White can calmly improve his
position and see how Magnus plans
to untangle.
15...♕c7 16.♔g1

16...♘b4 What to do? Castling
kingside seems scary, but Black has

Daniil Dubov jumps up in joy and Magnus Carlsen in horror, as 39.♕xf5 mate
throws the World Champion out of the Airthings Masters.

his resources and may hold. **17.♕c1
♖d8**

18.axb5 18.b3! was extremely strong,
as Vidit Gujrathi, guest commentator
for the day on one of the shows on
Chess24, quickly pointed out. Black's
queenside collapses. **18...cxb5
19.♗xb4** Dubov continues to look
for complications. 19.♗xb7 ♕xb7
20.♖xa5 equalizes the material score,
but it eases Magnus' defensive task.
**19...axb4 20.♖a7 ♘d5 21.♖g4
♖g8** I very much enjoyed Sachdev,
Leko and Vidit's live analyses on
Chess24, without a computer, of
course, and around here they were
spinning wildly to understand

what was going on. 21...♕b6 forces
22.♖xb7 ♕xb7 23.♖xg7, but I don't
think they saw any further. Amazingly, the computer gives equal play
here after 23...♖d7.

22.♕c2 Vidit, who again and again
impressed by spotting critical lines,
pointed out 22.♕b1!, with the idea
22...c3? 23.bxc3 bxc3 24.♕xb5+,
and White wins. Black can't stop
the queen invasion on h7, but he
can remove an enemy with 22...♖a8
and run with his queenside pawns.
The computer's evaluation is irrel-
evant here. In a practical game with
little time, it's a total mess. **22...c3
23.bxc3 bxc3**

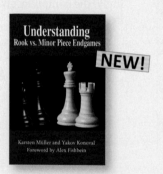

24.♖a3 Very surprising! Suddenly Dubov changes gear and starts withdrawing pieces. 24.♖f4 would have maintained the pressure. **24...♖c8 25.♘d3** Another retreat! **25...♘f6 26.♗xb7 ♕xb7**

27.♘c5?? Perhaps frustrated by his last two retreats, Dubov jumps forward again, but this is just a blunder. The obvious 27.♖h4 seems to hold the balance. **27...♖xc5 28.dxc5 ♘xg4 29.c6 ♕xc6** Black also has 29...♕b6 30.e3, and now 30...b4 31.♖a8+ ♔e7 32.♖xg8 b3, and the pawn queens. Magnus' choice is simpler. **30.♖xc3 ♕b6** Perhaps Dubov had overlooked the counterattack on f2. **31.e3**

31...♔e7! White has too little ammunition to punish the black king. **32.♖c6 ♕d8 33.♕c5+ ♔f6 34.♖d6**

34...♕e7?? Oh no! Suddenly everything changes. **35.♕d4+ ♔g5 36.f3!** With only seconds on the clock, Dubov is up to the task and grabs his chance.

36...f5 37.fxg4 ♖c8 There simply is no defence. 37...fxg4 38.♕e5 is mate. **38.♕f4+ ♔f6 39.♕xf5** Mate.

Ecstatic show

Norway is as chauvinistic as can be when it comes to sport. We worship our heroes like gods, but following this ecstatic show was fantastic TV entertainment even for total amateurs. Obviously the result was disappointing for the Norwegian audience, who had now found a new hero. However, against a practical and efficient Radjabov, Dubov didn't have a chance in the semi-final.

Then, in the match for third place – an innovation of the format – the heat was on again, when Dubov found his equal in Maxime Vachier-Lagrave. Dubov won the first two games on the first day, but MVL miraculously won the next two and equalled the score.

er 17...♛xb5 Stockfish's evaluation shot through the roof, but Maxime Vachier-Lagrave escaped (and even won) when Daniil Dubov didn't see how he could win on the spot.

The battle continued on the final day, now with MVL first taking the lead and then Dubov equalizing in Game 3. In the end, MVL won the fourth game and the match. Here's one of the highlights, MVL's miraculous last win on the first day, with which he levelled the score.

Daniil Dubov
Maxime Vachier-Lagrave
Airthings Masters 2020 (final 3rd place, 1.4)
Sicilian Defence, Moscow Variation

1.e4 c5 2.♘f3 d6 3.♗b5+ ♘d7 4.0-0 a6 5.♗xd7+ ♗xd7 6.c3 ♘f6 7.♖e1 ♗c6 8.d4!? It's all about initiative! **8...♗xe4 9.♗g5 ♗g6 10.d5 ♛d7 11.♘bd2 0-0-0 12.b4**

12...e6 12...♘xd5 13.♘c4 e6 14.♗xd8 ♛xd8 is an interesting exchange sacrifice, as seen in Delave-kouras-Keuter, ICCF 2014 (½-½).

13.♘c4 ♛b5 14.♘fd2

Some people simply love it messy! It's not easy to tell what's going on here. **14...exd5** 14...♘xd5 is supposed to be the only move holding the balance. **15.a4 ♛c6 16.b5 axb5 17.axb5 ♛xb5**

18.♛f3? The computer says 'game over', in White's favour, after the simple 18.♗xf6 gxf6 19.♘e3. **18... dxc4 19.♗xf6**

19...gxf6? Incredibly, 19...♖d7 seems to hold the balance. **20.♖a8+ ♔c7 21.♖xd8 ♔xd8 22.♛xf6+ ♔d7 23.♛xh8 ♗e7**

MVL has kind of managed to stabilize the position, but it's still highly unclear.

24.♘f1? Retreating doesn't suit Dubov. Here even the position screams for forwardness with either 24.f4 or 24.h4. The bishop on g6 needs to be challenged.
24...♛b6 25.♛a8 ♛a6 MVL finds an excellent plan aiming to exchange the queens.
26.♛h8 b5

27.♘e3
Again, going with the f- or h-pawn would have been more critical.

27...♕c8! The crisis is averted!
**28.♕xc8+ ♔xc8 29.♘xc4 ♔d8
30.♘a3 b4 31.cxb4 cxb4 32.♘c4
♔d7**

33.f3?! It's White who has to play
accurately to secure the draw, and
the next couple of moves are not
in accordance with the demands of
the position. **33...b3 34.♔f2 ♗f6
35.♘d2 b2 36.♘e4** It's lost anyway,
but this allows a clean Black win.

**36...♗xe4 37.fxe4 ♗g5 38.♖b1
♗c1 39.♔e2 ♔e6 40.♔d3 ♔e5
41.g3 h5 42.h3 f6 43.h4**

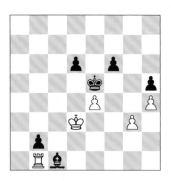

43...f5! It's like a pawn ending.
**44.exf5 ♔xf5 45.♔d4 ♔g4
46.♔d5 ♔xg3 47.♔xd6 ♔xh4
48.♔e5 ♔g3** White resigned.

Good air matters

Airthings, the main sponsor of this
leg, is a manufacturer of equipment
to measure indoor air quality. It was
an interesting novelty to have the air
quality in the players' rooms measured
and shown. Would there be a correla-
tion between the 'radon level' in the
room and the player's performance?
There seems to be every reason to
believe there is. The commentators
pointed out that the air quality in Anish
Giri's office was below par, and he had
a meagre result in the preliminaries.
On the other hand, Maxime Vachier-
Lagrave was scoring very well both 'on
the board' and on the air quality around
him.

During the 2018 Fischer Random
World Championship final between
Wesley So and Magnus Carlsen, the
players' heart rate was measured. It was
revealing to see the enormous calmness
inside Magnus, while Wesley seemed

Would there be a correlation between the 'radon level' in the room and the player's performance?

to be running on full speed all the way.
One might think that keeping your
cool would be good, but it actually was
Wesley who won the match convincingly. Good air quality seems to be an
undeniable boon, however, and perhaps
something we will think about more in
the near future.

Another factor in these global online
events is the time zone from which you
play. While Magnus at his undisclosed
location (the Seychelles) sat down at his
computer in the early evening, Hikaru
Nakamura's day at the office started
very early in the morning, which is quite
unusual for chess players. Normally
speaking, the American is one of the hot
favourites in these events, but we saw
very little of his normal qualities this

time. He did qualify for the knock-
out stage, but then was knocked out
'without a fight' by Levon Aronian.

**NOTES BY
Anish Giri**

**Levon Aronian
Hikaru Nakamura**
Airthings 2020 (qf 2.1)
Queen's Pawn Opening, London System

1.d4 ♘f6 2.♘f3 d5 3.♗f4 The
London System is always an option!
3...e6 4.e3 ♗d6 One of the most
solid set-ups Black has.
5.♘bd2 c5
Many move orders are possible here.
This one allows White to give a check,
which Levon Aronian duly does.
**6.♗b5+ ♘c6 7.♗xc6+ bxc6
8.♗xd6 ♕xd6 9.♘b3**

White has traded a couple of minor
pieces and goes for dark-square
control – a very ambitious approach,
but things aren't that simple, and
Black fights back, of course.
9...cxd4 10.exd4 ♘d7
A decent move, guarding the
c5-square and preparing for the
eventual ...f6-e5 push.
11.♕d2 Hinting at thoughts about
castling queenside.
11...0-0 12.♕c3
The queen reinforces its control of the
dark squares before White castles.
12...f6!
Stopping ♘e5 and preparing ...e5,
challenging White's central control.
13.0-0-0

Yes, 22.f4 is coming. Rapid ace Hikaru Nakamura was unrecognizable and lost 'without a fight' in the quarter finals to Levon Aronian (1½-2½ and 0-2).

Now ♖a3 is a threat, so Black has to lose extra time defending a7.
19...♖a8 Sad, but it was all hopeless already anyway.
20.♘d4 e5

21.♘f5
Obviously not going for the c6-pawn, which would yield nothing, but penetrating on d6 with the knight.
21...♖ed8 22.f4!
Undermining the dark squares.
22...♗c8

23.♘d6+ Cashing in.
23...♖xd6 24.cxd6 e4

25.c4! Black's central pawns are going nowhere, and White gets to defend the d6-soldier.
25...♔e6 26.c5

13...♗a6?!
The immediate e5-push would have been better: 13...e5! would have given Black fine play in the centre. Now advances like ...a5 and ...c5 are in the air: 14.dxe5 fxe5 15.♖he1 ♖e8, and White can't quite exploit the fact that Black's rooks aren't connected.
14.♖he1 ♖fe8 15.♖e3
Intending to double on the e-file.

15...♖ac8
But this is already really odd. Black should have started some desperately needed counterplay with 15...e5!, followed by ...e4, grabbing space in the centre and creating counterplay.
16.♖de1 ♔f7 Getting the king closer to the e6-pawn. Perhaps Hikaru Nakamura realized that the ...c5-push would be impossible otherwise.
The immediate 16...c5 is met by 17.dxc5 ♘xc5 18.♘xc5 ♖xc5 19.♖xe6!, and the tactics work for White.
17.♘c5 ♘xc5

18.♕xc5!
Good judgement. The endgame is great for White, since he gets to blockade the dark squares.
18...♕xc5 19.dxc5

The rest is a matter of technique.
White's protected passer is a step
further than Black's, and White is
also up an exchange.
26...♗a6 27.♖a3 Levon breaks
through on the queenside.
27...♗b5 28.b4 ♔f5

29.♖a5 A great plan, followed by a
well-timed a4-b5 push.
29...♗c4 30.a4 a6

31.g4+!? Deflecting the king
further in order to accommodate the
queenside breakthrough.
31...♔xf4 32.b5 cxb5 33.c6 ♔e5
The king is now one step too far away
to be able to stop the pawn.

34.c7 ♔e6
Since 34...♔xd6 35.♖xa6+ is curtains.

35.♖xa6 And Hikaru resigned.
If he defends with 35...♖c8, the
easiest reply would be 36.a5, followed
by ♖b6, the march of the a-pawn, and
♖b8. Black has no counterplay at all.

■ ■ ■

Thanks to Play Magnus for another
great event, and thanks to the players
for putting up the show. And particularly thanks to those that show us that
even the very best make mistakes –
which will perhaps make it easier for
us to accept our own stupidities.

Nakamura-Aronian
Airthings Masters 2020 (qf 2.2)
position after 24...♗b7

25.a5? ♘g4+! **26.fxg4 ♗xh1** and
with an exchange up, Black won easily
(0-1, 34 moves).

Radjabov-Nepomniachtchi
Airthings Masters 2020 (qf 2.1)
position after 18.♖ac1

18...♕b7?
Black seems to be under pressure, but
after almost any other queen move
this would have been remedied.
19.♕e4! g6 20.♗xh6
and White won a crucial pawn and
eventually the game (1-0, 32). ■

Fair & Square

Anya Taylor-Joy: 'It was important for me to honour the chess community and understand what I was doing. But I also likened Beth's passion for chess to my passion for acting. It's a calling. You answer it. Then you become obsessed and spend the rest of your life figuring out how to get better at it.' *(After being selected as one of the Observer's 'Faces of 2020', following her acclaimed performance as Beth Harmon in The Queen's Gambit)*

Michael Ball: 'I've done a hungover show before and vowed to never do it again. The last time was after the last night of *CHESS*, when I got in drunk at 4 a.m. and realized I still had to do the show.' *(The singer interviewed by the Guardian)*

George R.R. Martin: 'It also resonated with me very strongly. I know that world. Chess was a huge part of my life in high school, in college, and especially in the years after college, the early 70s. *The Queen's Gambit* brought it all back to me vividly.' *(The author and creator of Game of Thrones in his blog)*

Waldemar Januszczak: 'Chess. If you poured a bucket of Drambuie down me and span me 1,000 times, I still could not have imagined that the focus of the latest hit on Netflix, the main topic in the chat rooms of WhatsApp this week, would be chess.' *(The broadcaster and art critic for The Sunday Times, in his column of November 30)*

Garry Kasparov: 'She did not teach me what I should think, but that I should have a critical attitude to everything that I read or heard.' *(On his mother Klara, who sadly died of Covid-19 on Christmas Day, aged 83)*

Klara Kasparova: 'If not you, who else?' *(The handwritten note Garry Kasparov's mother placed on her 10-year-old son's bed to inspire him to greatness)*

Judit Polgar: 'I think it would be a much bigger breakthrough to have three ladies in the top ten, than to have a world champion who is a lady.' *(In an interview in Euronews following the runaway success of Netflix's The Queen's Gambit)*

Jennifer Shahade: 'Chess demands your whole mind. It's a meditative experience that people are really craving right now.'*(Answering in the media why chess has become a popular pastime online and on TV during the pandemic)*

Demis Hassabis: 'Instead of pitching him my business idea, I tried to intrigue him. In that one minute, I managed to crowbar in the question of why chess is such an amazing game. I have asked grandmasters this question and they have struggled to give an answer. But as a game designer, I have thought deeply about it. Chess is exquisite. It is almost perfectly balanced.' *(After months agonis-*

ing over his pitch, the co-founder of DeepMind explains in The Sunday Times of December 6 how he managed to get chess-playing billionaire tech investor Peter Thiel to 'take notice' of his start-up AI lab)*

Jo Ellison: 'Even some proximity to chess makes us feel intelligent, sophisticated, and seductive.' *(In her Financial Times column of 28 November, on the appeal and success of The Queen's Gambit)*

Alexander Yermolinsky: 'Asking chess players about their rating is bad taste; it's like asking a woman about her age.' *(The former US champion in the Chess24 chat during the Airthings Masters semifinals)*

Björk: 'Chess is massive in Iceland. There's a lot of chess-playing and telling stories while you're getting hilariously drunk. Falling asleep on the chess table is very much part of Icelandic culture.' *(The Icelandic pop icon, interviewed in 1994 by Hot Press, on the release of Debut, her first international solo album)*

Stanley Kubrick: 'I don't suppose you want moronic-logic-of-the-audience feedback on any plot points: so none offered. Kasparov does not need the comments of the kibitzers.' *(Following the recent death of John le Carré, a note from 1992 was released by the film director's estate, that thanked the spy novelist for sending him a signed advanced copy of The Tailor of Panama)*

Finding Beth Harmon

Did Walter Tevis have Diana Lanni in mind when he wrote *The Queen's Gambit*?

Diana Lanni

Beth Harmon

Was Beth Harmon, the leading character in the incredibly popular Netflix series *The Queen's Gambit*, based on a real life person? **LARRY KAUFMAN** has little doubt and builds a strong case for American chess player Diana Lanni. And he also believes to know who was the inspiration for Beth's first real trainer Harry Beltik.

Beth Harmon, the American chess genius in the Netflix series *The Queen's Gambit* and the 1983 novel by Walter Tevis on which it was based, is a fictional character. The 1960s time frame during which she achieved her chess successes pretty well mirror Bobby Fischer's achievements, but no female chess player was a serious threat to the male world champions at the time. The few women who did achieve some success against grandmasters before 1983, notably Vera Menchik, Nona Gaprindashvili, and Maya Chiburdanidze, all born in Russia or the Soviet Union, had very little in common with the Beth Harmon character aside from chess prowess and gender. Beth Harmon was on her own in life from her late teens, was an alcoholic and had a drug problem, was prone to severe depression, and remained a loner until the end of the book and series. I don't believe any of this applied to any of the above-mentioned women.

So, did Walter Tevis just make all this up? Not really. To begin with there are evident autobiographical elements. Tevis was confined to a hospital when he was 10. His parents moved to another town. At that age, most children would feel abandoned and liken it to being orphaned. Just like Beth Harmon at the orphanage, Tevis was drugged by the staff at the hospital, leading to a life of struggles with addiction. Then, once Beth is adopted at age 15, her life shows many similarities with another person from the real world, Diana Lanni.

Tevis must have known Diana Lanni, as they frequented the same chess haunts. Just like him, Lanni regularly played in Washington Square Park in the early 80s when Tevis was working on his book. She was also a frequent visitor of the Game Room, which was owned and run by Stuart Morden. In the preface to his book, Tevis thanks Morden for his help, along with Bruce Pandolfini ('all excellent chess players'), who also knew Lanni. Either or both of them, or many of the regular players there, could have given Tevis whatever info he needed for the book, since Lanni was not a secretive person and would tell her story and problems readily. Her blitz games at these two chess sites always drew large crowds, which Tevis would have surely observed.

The Game Room had a bar, where Lanni drank, nightly. With Tevis' drinking problem, they probably conversed at this bar. Lanni often played the jukebox and danced, which Tevis could observe. Drinking caused enormous changes in personality in both Beth and Lanni: they both were reserved, anxious people, who could only let go of their inhibitions when they drank.

Walking into a chess club

Diana Lanni learned chess as a child from her father, a rated Expert player (2000-2199) in Washington, D.C. Beth Harmon learned chess at age 8 from the janitor at the orphanage in Kentucky, who became her 'father figure' and whom she described after his death as a 'strong player'. Diana's father, an alcoholic who molested her, apparently didn't

even teach her much about chess beyond the rules. Similarly Beth Harmon was abandoned by both her real father and her adoptive father, neither of whom cared at all for her well-being. Both were left with no parents in their life after their late teens. Diana's parents divorced and had only minimal further contact

Beth Harmon and Diana Lanni both were reserved, anxious people, who could only let go of their inhibitions when they drank

with her until she reconnected with her ailing elderly mother in recent years. Beth's two mothers both died and she had no friendly contact with her two fathers.

At the age of 19, in early 1975, Diana Lanni was taking art classes in a building out in Silver Spring, Maryland, and noticed that there was a chess club in the same building. She decided to check it out, and came in one day. I was the club manager

Larry Kaufman and Diana Lanni, probably in 1977, when she came back to Miami to visit him.

and asked whom she was looking for, since attractive young women didn't normally play in chess clubs back then. Well, there had been one notable exception, Lisa Lane (born in 1938), who had been US Women's Champion in 1959. She was a media sensation due to her youth and beauty, although she was never rated much above 2000, but she left chess in the mid-60s.

As she walked into the club, I was quite surprised when Diana said that she was there to play chess. It took only a very short time to determine that she was a rank novice, maybe 600 Elo level, she couldn't even win with something like a queen and two rooks handicap from me. But she was determined to become a good player, and we quickly became close. I was a National Master then, 8 years older than she.

Now switch to Beth Harmon. Her first contact with tournament chess was at the age of 15, where she met (and defeated) Harry Beltik in Kentucky. Beltik was eight years older than Beth, and became a National Master soon after the event. He was a recent Kentucky champion, I was a recent Maryland champion. He became her first real teacher and they lived together for a limited time while he taught her what he could about chess. It was the same with Diana and me, except that Beth was already master strength when living with Beltik, whereas Diana only reached 1300-1400 level during our initial time together.

At the time I had a standing offer to go into the stock options business in Miami with a former chess student who was a wealthy rare coin dealer, but I was very reluctant to move to

I never heard of anyone playing at novice level at age 19 who became a master

Miami where I would know no one other than him. But Diana was very keen to get away from the DC area and was thrilled with the idea and persuaded me that we should move there together. And so I resigned my job running the chess club for famous tournament organizer Bill Goichberg.

In Miami we got an apartment from my options partner, who owned a whole apartment building there. I had little income for the six months or so it took to learn everything I needed to learn about options and to develop formulae for trading them. Diana helped me with collecting data on stock prices to use for the models I developed. We worked on chess regularly. I recall playing handicap games with her, as I normally do with students. I think her handicap then was rook plus knight. I must admit that I couldn't imagine that she would ever become a master, not because of her gender but because I never heard of anyone playing at novice level at age 19 who became a master.

Then Diana took a job as a dancer at a rather seedy bar, which was a big mistake. Just like Beth Harmon, she became an alcoholic, got hooked on various drugs (I never even knew the details), and smoked cigarettes. Just like Harry Beltik, I never drank much alcohol or smoked or had any drug problems, but like Harry, I was unable to change her behaviour in these matters.

It was clear that this wasn't working out and Diana felt that she needed to leave Miami to get away from some very dangerous men she had worked with. So, very soon after my business started to prosper, she was gone. I immediately gave up chess one hundred per cent to focus on my career, exactly as Harry Beltik did when separating from Beth Harmon. I returned to chess after three years, while Beltik returned to chess to help Harmon with her crucial adjournment against the World Champion, Vasily Borgov.

Stunning improvement

Diana ended up in Ann Arbor, Michigan, where she went to college, doing quite well there for three years, with a 3.8 G.P.A. with plans to go to law school. We stayed in touch and she came down to Miami to visit me twice during that period. Similarly Beth Harmon and Harry Beltik remained friends long after they no longer lived together. In 1979 I married Sandra Swartz, with whom I had two children. At the same time, Diana lost her financial aid due to a

Diana Lanni loved to go out and have a drink. It helped her to unwind, but also got her into trouble.

bureaucratic snafu and had to drop out without a degree, which led to a life of continual financial need and the constant threat or reality of homelessness.

She had improved considerably in chess during those years, to class A level, but this was of course not enough to make money from chess. In 1979 Diana got invited to the US Women's championship, which back then only required a rating of around 1800. Although she finished near

the bottom, as expected, this can be considered the start of her real chess career. In 1980, she visited the famous Lone Pine masters tournament where I had one of my best lifetime results, an even score vs 7 GMs (plus draws vs. two IMs). Diana began to live and travel with the late famous backgammon champion and writer Paul Magriel, who had been a successful chess player as a junior but switched games when rated around 2000. Although this only lasted around six months, she learned backgammon and continued to work on chess. She thus ended up in New York, Magriel's hometown, and stayed there to devote most of her time to chess. Around 1981 she won the women's championships of both the Marshall and Manhattan chess clubs in New York, the two most prestigious chess clubs in the nation.

Near the end of 1981 she had herself committed to the mental health wing of Bellevue Hospital in New York for about a month. Soon after release, she resumed playing both tournament and blitz chess, and saw her USCF rating published at about 2185. She was tied for second among US Women and near the magic 2200 needed for the US Master title (not based on gender, unlike FIDE titles).

She entered a 'Futurity' invitational round-robin tournament and did well enough to comfortably pass the required 2200. She drew with soon-to-be GM Sergey Kudrin, while Earl Hall, an FM then rated 2345, reports that he was lucky to get a draw against her. She also beat the tournament director whose FIDE rating around that time was 2370. But the tournament director never sent the event in for rating because he lost his own game to Lanni and had a poor result.

Diana stopped playing rated chess, waiting for several months for the master rating to be published before resuming play, but the rating never appeared, and she eventually gave up on chess as a serious career. But she did play second board for the US Women's team in the 1982 Olympiad in Lucerne, where she drew her game playing Black against the Soviet women's champion and former Women's World Champion GM Nona Gaprindashvili.

Nona Gaprindashvili
Diana Lanni
Lucerne Olympiad 1982
Tarrasch Defence

1.c4 e6 2.♘f3 d5 3.d4 c5 4.cxd5 exd5 5.g3 ♘c6 6.♗c3 ♘f6 7.♗g2 ♗e7 8.0-0 0-0 9.♗g5 cxd4 10.♘xd4 h6 11.♗e3 ♖e8 12.♕a4

12...♘e5?! 13.♘xd5?!
After 13.♕b3 ♘c4 14.♖ad1 ♘xe3 15.fxe3 White should win a pawn, but Black will have some compensation.
13...♘xd5 14.♗xd5
Diana admitted that she was out of book and simply had overlooked on move 12 that the bishop could not be taken now due to the hanging rook on e8, but actually, as the continuation shows, it wasn't such a bad sacrifice.
14...♗h3 15.♗g2 ♗xg2 16.♔xg2

16...♕d5+?!
After 16...♘g4 17.♗c1 ♗c5 18.♘f3 ♘f6 19.e3 ♘e4 Black has much better development for the pawn.
17.♘f3 ♘c4?! 18.♖ad1?
After 18.♗d4! ♗g5 19.♕d1 Black has only slight compensation for the pawn.
18...♘xe3+ 19.fxe3 ♕e6 20.♖d7 ♗c5 21.e4

White had little time left and a draw was agreed in view of the following sequence: 21...♕xe4 22.♕xe4 ♖xe4 23.♘g1 ♖e7 24.♖xe7 ♗xe7 25.♖c1

♗d6 and with bishop for knight in an open position and better pawn structure, Black is for choice in a drawish endgame.

When I heard about this game, I was truly impressed. I could not have imagined that a 19-year-old who was no stronger than Elo 600, would seven years later draw a game as Black against Nona Gaprindashvili, who had been Women's World Champion for 16 of the preceding 20 years! And she did it despite minimal knowledge of opening theory. To this day she only knows the names of a few openings. For this reason she has recently preferred to play Chess960 (or Fischerandom) online.

Poker and prison
So Diana Lanni earned (but didn't receive) her National Master title about the same time as Walter Tevis was writing *The Queen's Gambit*, and he probably imagined that she

The evidence that Diana Lanni was the inspiration for Beth Harmon is mostly circumstantial, but rather overwhelming

would go on to much greater achievements. Unfortunately this was not to be, this was her high-water mark. She gradually lost interest in chess over the next few years. While living at Bill Goichberg's Chess Center in Manhattan, she was badly injured in a skating 'accident' (in quotes because she says it was a deliberate attack by a stranger). Sitting became very painful for her, and while she continued to play with diminishing frequency, she eventually gave it up.

Around 1985 Diana Lanni took up poker, learning originally mostly from books, but later getting advice from Magriel, who had become a top poker player and with whom she remained good friends. She became good enough to make a living from poker, as a player and later as a dealer, for about a decade. Probably she got to be stronger at poker than at chess. She was very good at the skill of 'reading' people, which is not a big part of chess.

At various times from 1979 to 1996, Lanni worked at various jobs in the sports betting industry. While sports betting is now legal in 18 states with the number climbing rapidly, back then it was only legal in Nevada, but she worked in New York until about 1984 and in California after that. In 1996 she was arrested for running the office of a sports betting company on the wrong side of the California-Nevada border, and in 1999 was sentenced to 8 months in federal prison.

While I don't condone lawbreaking, this seems a bit harsh for such a minor offense, and given the current legal acceptance of sports betting I think she is much more deserving of a presidential pardon than so many others who have gotten one. She is an ethical person, but has had to cut corners in life after missing out on both her

college degree and the master title in chess through no fault of her own.

After the prison term she worked in health care and teaching girls to play chess, until a second injury forced her onto disability. Despite her own health issues, she is still taking care of her elderly mother.

Her last US Chess rated standard event was in 2001, and her last Quick rated event in 2014. She recently resumed playing chess online on chess.com as LanaCaprini.

This Olympiad photo of Diana Lanni may have inspired Walter Tevis to write: 'Beth leaned over the table, digging her fists into her cheeks, and tried to penetrate the position.'

The evidence that Diana Lanni was the inspiration for Beth Harmon is mostly circumstantial, but rather overwhelming. I think it is pretty clear that Lanni played a role in formulating the character and the story. Just how big a role is the question. There is no 'smoking gun' to prove the case conclusively, although the description of Beth Harmon in the book, 'Beth leaned

over the table, digging her fists into her cheeks, and tried to penetrate the position' sure sounds like it was based on the Olympiad photo of Diana.

If we accept that Diana was a prime inspiration for Beth Harmon, and that I would be the closest match to Harry Beltik (if only by coincidence), who is Benny Watts based on? The conventional answer is Bobby Fischer, but to me the character seems much more like the late Walter Browne. Watts was portrayed as a five-times US Champion but not in the same league with the top Soviet players. Furthermore Watts was portrayed as a fairly normal, if somewhat conceited and brash, young man, who excelled at blitz and was willing to admit that Beth was his superior in chess and willing to help her with the crucial adjournment.

This all sounds much more like Walter than like Bobby. I knew Walter pretty well, and despite his reputation he was a pretty nice guy with his friends, and would probably have helped out too in that situation. Also he knew Lanni well, and was close to my age just as Watts and Beltik are supposed to be the same age. And we know that Tevis met Walter Browne and described him vividly in his article on the 1974 National Open in *The Atlantic Monthly* (see New In Chess 2020/8).

Of course, since Watts is fictional, there is no right answer. Undoubtedly both Fischer and Browne helped mould the character. I claim that Browne was the greater influence. Just as Diana Lanni was not the sole influence for Beth Harmon, but she was probably the most important one. ∎

This article is an adapted chapter from Larry Kaufman's forthcoming memoir Chess Board Options (New In Chess, 2021). Diana Lanni contributed to the article – writing and rewriting a few of the more personal lines in the story, especially regarding her father – and approves of its contents.

Thomas Willemze

Club players, test your decision-making skills!

What would you play?

Obtaining an advantage is one thing, converting it quite another. How do you remain in charge and stop your opponent from breaking free?

One of the most frustrating experiences in chess is a game in which you feel you are ruling the board, but are unable to turn this into anything concrete. By the time you realize this, your advantage has evaporated, and you are just in time to witness how your opponent has already taken over.

Exercises

This scenario occurred in the game between Kanwal Bhatia (2037) and David Latham (2064), played in the 4NCL in 2020. White got a comfortable position right from the start, but did not have a clear path towards victory available. In four exercises, we will put ourselves in his shoes and demonstrate that patiently depriving your opponent of his defensive resources is an effective technique to convert an advantage.

Exercise 1

position after 22...♗c6

White's active knight and doubled rooks put him clearly in charge. His next step, however, is unclear. **How**

would you continue?** Would you focus on the kingside with 23.g3, or on the queenside with 23.b4 ?

Exercise 2

position after 25...♕e7

Black is about to relieve the pressure on his position. Can you see how? **What would you play to prevent it?**

Exercise 3

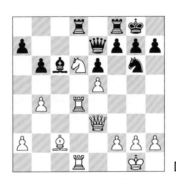

position after 27...f6

Black is challenging the important e5-pawn and is on his way to generating serious counterplay. What should White do to stay in charge? **What would you play?**

Exercise 4

position after 34...♕e5

Black has moved his queen into the centre and is about to turn his counterplay into a very serious threat. **How would you stop him?**

I hope you enjoyed these exercises and were able to restrict Black's defensive resources. You can find the full analysis of this game on the following pages.

Patiently depriving your opponent of his defensive resources is an effective technique to convert an advantage

Kanwal Bhatia (2037)
David Latham (2064)
Daventry 2020
Caro-Kann, Smyslov Variation

**1.e4 c6 2.d4 d5 3.♘d2 dxe4
4.♘xe4 ♘d7 5.♘f3 ♘df6 6.♘g3**

6...e6
Black's light-squared bishop becomes very passive after this move, which is why Black should have moved it outside the pawn chain first with 6...♗g4. Black does not mind trading this bishop for the knight after, for instance, 7.c3 e6 8.h3 ♗xf3 9.♕xf3.

ANALYSIS DIAGRAM

The black pawns and the remaining bishop complement each other nicely, and Black's pawn formation is solid enough the withstand the pressure from the white bishop pair.

White gets a comfortable position but does not have a clear path towards victory available

**7.♗d3 ♗d6 8.0-0 ♘e7 9.♖e1 0-0
10.♘e5**

If you compare this strong knight with Black's passive light-squared bishop, you can imagine that a trade would have been a good deal for Black.
**10...♘g6 11.♗g5 ♗e7 12.c3
♘d5 13.♗xe7 ♕xe7 14.♗c2**

14...♘xe5
It makes a lot of sense to eliminate the dominant e5-knight, but this trade enables White to create a powerful outpost for his knight with the recapturing d-pawn. I would therefore prefer 14...♖d8, followed by ...♗d7-e8, and eventually ...c6-c5 to open up the position for the black pieces.
**15.dxe5 ♘f4 16.♕d4 ♘g6
17.♖ad1 b6**

18.♘e4
White keeps making simple and strong moves. An interesting alternative would have been the bold 18.♗xg6, since both recapturing moves by Black have distinct drawbacks.
18...hxg6 would open up the h-file to the black king. The game might continue with 19.♕g4 ♗b7 20.♘e4 ♖ad8 21.♘d6.

ANALYSIS DIAGRAM

White will follow-up with ♖e3-h3, with a dangerous attack.
18...fxg6 deprives Black of the undermining ...f7-f6 break. We can already see the consequences after 19.♘e4 ♗b7 20.♘d6. Black can no longer challenge White's e5-pawn, and must accept this knight as a long-term thorn in his flesh.
**18...♗b7 19.♘d6 ♖ad8 20.♕e3
♗a8**

21.♖d2
White patiently increases the pressure on the d-file. Note that ♗xg6, as discussed above, was again possible, but not necessary. White keeps improving his position and saves the big decisions for later.

21...c5 22.罝ed1 象c6

We have arrived at **Exercise 1**, which is an important moment in the game. So far, White has been able to improve his pieces without much resistance. Now he is ready for the next step, which involves creating a second weakness. The big question is: where?

23.b4 The correct answer was: the kingside! White could start with 23.g3 and build up an attack with, for instance, h4-h5. It is important to note that Black can only survive if he generates enough counterplay. His best chance would be a well-timed ...f7-f6, but this would weaken his pawn structure considerably.

23...cxb4 24.cxb4

In my book *The Chess Toolbox*, I describe two important defensive tools in the fight for an open file: Blocking the file and opening up an additional file to generate counter-play. White's 23.b4 presented both goals on a silver platter to Black. First, Black can now block the open file with 24...象d5!, threatening ...公xe5!, since he no longer has to fear c3-c4. Second, he can use the second open

file to finally activate his rook with ...罝d7-c7.

24...豐h4 Black does not seize the opportunity, but will get a second chance soon. **25.罝d4 豐e7**

I have already revealed the answer to **Exercise 2**. Black is ready to block the open file with 26...象d5, and White must prevent this with 26.象b3!. Next, he will start his king-side attack with 27.豐g3 and 28.h4. Note that 26...罝d7 would run into 27.b5 象a8

ANALYSIS DIAGRAM

28.公f5!. This discovered attack wins the exchange.
26.a3 象d5!

Black grabs his second chance. White

is still better, but only if he manages to keep e5 under control.
27.f4 Well played! The knight on d6 can relax again. **27...f6**

This is the principled move, trying to destabilize the knight. White has to be very precise if he wants to stay in control. The correct solution to **Exercise 3** was 28.豐h3!, intending to meet 28...fxe5 with 29.象xg6!. White threatens 30.豐xh7 mate, forcing Black to recapture: 29...hxg6 30.fxe5.

ANALYSIS DIAGRAM

With the e5-pawn secured and 罝h4 in the air, White is very close to winning.
28.豐g3

Now Black can finally get rid of the annoying white knight.

THE NEW CHESSBASE DATABASES 2021

ChessBase

MEGA DATABASE 2021

8,4 million games
85,300 annotated games

INCLUSIVE 250,000 new games in 2021 ONLINE UPDATE

MEGA DATABASE 2021

DVD

From Carlsen to Mamedyarov – with analysis by all current top ten players!

The ChessBase Mega Database 2021, with over 8.3 million games from between 1560 and 2020, is the exclusive chess database which meets the highest demands. With over 85 000 annotated games Mega 2021 contains the world's largest collection of top class analysed games. Train like a pro! With ChessBase 16 and the Mega Database 2021 prepare yourself for your opponent with great precision, let grandmasters explain the best way to play your favourite variations, improve your repertoire and much more.

- Including Mega Update Service 2021: week by week bring your Mega up to date with your ChessBase 15/16 program with over 5 000 new games, that is approx. 250 000 new games by the end of 2021!
- New design, easier to use! Direct access to the games of the world championships and the great tournaments of the history of chess, and much more.
- Download a player encyclopaedia with over 586 000 names of players and over 40 000 photos of players (only with ChessBase 14/15/16)

Mega Database 2021*	**€ 189.90**
Update from Mega Database 2020	**€ 69.90**
Update from older Mega Database	**€ 119.90**

Big Database 2021
The ChessBase database without annotations and analyses.
8.3 million games from between 1560 and 2020.
Without update service.

Big Database 2021*	**€ 69.90**

NEW: Fritz Powerbook 2021

Complete opening theory in an all-embracing opening book. That is the Fritz Powerbook 2021. With over 25 million positions including statistics concerning frequency, success rate etc. the Powerbook is the most important supplement to your Fritz program! Ideal for learning and studying your own variations and for practising them.

Also supplied with: a collection of the 1.5 million top level games from which the Powerbook 2021 was constructed as well as the special book "Strongbook", generated from the strongest grandmaster games (ELO >= 2550) of the last hundred years (over 2 million positions).

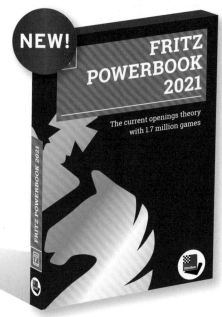

NEW!

FRITZ POWERBOOK 2021

The current openings theory with 1.7 million games

FRITZ POWERBOOK 2021

Fritz Powerbook 2021*	**€ 69.90**
Update from Powerbook 2020	**€ 39.90**

* Available from 17.11.2020

Online Shop: shop.chessbase.com · ChessBase GmbH · Osterbekstr. 90a · 22083 Hamburg · Germany · info@chessbase.com
CHESSBASE DEALER: NEW IN CHESS · P.O. Box 1093 · NL-1810 KB Alkmaar · phone (+31)72 5127137 · fax (+31)72 5158234 · WWW.NEWINCHESS.COM

28...fxe5! 29.fxe5 ♞xe5 30.♕xe5 ♕xd6

White definitely has compensation for the pawn, but must be careful in his attack because his opponent is no longer a passive bystander.
31.♕h5 h6 32.♕g6

32...♖f6 I would have preferred 32...♕e5!, since counterattack is the best defence! Nothing beats a centralized queen in combining defensive and offensive duties.
33.♕h7+ ♚f8 34.♗g6 ♕e5

35.♕h8+ This move leads White into a dead-end street, with fatal consequences.
35.♖e4! was the only solution to **Exercise 4.** The rook uses the pin to expel the centralized black queen. After 35...♕c3 36.h3! White is ready to let the tactics work in his favour, e.g. 36...♚e7 37.♕xg7+ ♚d6 38.♖dd4.

ANALYSIS DIAGRAM

A beautiful picture! The f6-rook is unable to move due to the discovered attack that arises after 39.♖xd5+!. If Black defends the rook with 38...♖df8, White crashes through with 39.♖xd5+!

ANALYSIS DIAGRAM

39...exd5 (39...♚xd5 40.♕d7 is mate!) 40.♕e7+ ♚c6 41.♗e8+! ♖xe8 42.♕xe8+ ♚b7 43.♖e7+ ♚a6 44.♕a4, mate.
Note that 35.h3 (or 35.h4) is only a draw after 35...♕e3+

ANALYSIS DIAGRAM

36.♚h2 (36.♚h1 ♕xh3+!) 36...♕e5+

Nothing beats a centralized queen in combining defensive and offensive duties

37.♚g1 (37.♚h1 ♗xg2+!) 37...♕e3+ with a perpetual.
35...♚e7 36.♕xg7+ ♚d6

White has run out of checks and can no longer defend against both 37...♖f1+! and 37...♕e2!.
37.♕h7 ♕e2! 38.♖4d2 ♕e3+!

39.♚h1 ♕xd2
Taking the queen would lead to a back-rank mate, which is why White resigned.

This game provides us a few important defensive tools, e.g. blocking an open file and developing counterplay. It also demonstrated how impatience in converting one's advantage can easily backfire, and that one should focus on limiting the opponent's possibilities before designing a long-term plan to decide the game. ∎

The Russian Super Final was a wonderful treat. Clearly delighted to be back at the board, the players laid into each other with great gusto and creativity. A tense neck-and-neck race between Ian Nepomniachtchi and Sergey Karjakin was only decided on the final day. Daniil Dubov brilliantly defeated both frontrunners, but paid for his risky play in other key games. **VLADIMIR BARSKY** reports from the Russian capital.

Tight race in Moscow

Nepomniachtchi edges out Karjakin to clinch Russian title

The Super Final of the Russian Championship is the most prestigious tournament on the internal calendar, bringing together almost all the strongest grandmasters of the country. It is also the most elegant one, since it is part of the Chess in Museums programme and is always held at splendid venues. But 2020 was a special year, and until late autumn we did not know whether it would take place at all.

Until the end of the summer, everyone sat at home and played only on the Internet. The first major in-person tournament was held in September – in Chelyabinsk, where the organizers had to fulfil dozens, if not hundreds of requirements in view of the pandemic. But the main thing was that the competition took place at all, and that it ended without incident! In the wake of this success, it was possible to hold the qualifier for the Super Final, the so-called First League, in Sochi.

The Super Final was held in Moscow, in the Central Chess Club on Gogolevsky Boulevard, which is also the home of the Russian Chess Federation and the Chess Museum. In the capital, the situation as regards medicines is clearly better than in the provinces, and in your own building it is easier to provide all the necessary precautions. Let's list the main ones. Two to three days before the start and after six of the 11 rounds, all participants, arbiters, journalists, video broadcasters, security guards, cleaners, etc., had a Covid test. Before the start of each round, the temperature of the chess players was measured twice: on the first floor, opposite the entrance door to the building, and on the second floor, before the entrance to the playing hall. From the beginning to the end of each round, a doctor was on duty. Transparent plexi-glass screens were installed on the playing tables, and there were no handshakes before or after the games. Some chess players preferred to play with masks, and hand sanitizers were literally everywhere. Unfortunately but understandably, spectators were not allowed.

The field was impressive, with only a few absentees. The 2019 Champion, Evgeny Tomashevsky, declined to participate and stayed at home to support his wife, who was expecting their first child. For personal reasons, Alexander Grischuk and Dmitry Andreikin did not play either.

The chess we were about to witness was just fascinating. It was evident that the grandmasters had missed playing 'live', and in the over-

Ian Nepomniachtchi watches the key game between Daniil Dubov and Sergey Karjakin in the last round of the Super Final.

whelming majority of games they strove to fight to the last bullet.

'Finally I played a game of classical chess after a whole year of preparation!' tweeted Sergey Karjakin, accompanying his post with a photo of the festively illuminated façade of the Central Chess Club and a bunch of emoticons. Sergey beat debutant Mikhail Antipov with black in his trademark active positional style (which, frankly speaking, we had started forgetting about a little bit in recent years), refuting his opponent's risky play.

'Finally I played a game of classical chess after a whole year of preparation!' tweeted Sergey Karjakin

Mikhail Antipov
Sergey Karjakin
Moscow 2020 (1)

position after 12...♖f7

Black has successfully solved his opening problems, and now his position is at least not worse. However, after the natural 13.0-0 ♖af8 (13...a5!?) 14.b4 White wouldn't have had anything to worry about either. However, Mikhail Antipov is very fond of 'adventure' chess, and he decided to improve his position.
13.h4 ♖af8 14.b4 As one of the classics said: to attack on two flanks

at once, you need two sets of pieces. In fact, with the help of b2-b4, Mikhail only wants to clear the second rank for transferring the a1-rook to the centre, but in the long term, his queenside becomes 'loose'.
14...♔h8 15.♖a2 ♗d8!
A subtle manoeuvre: Black not only increases the pressure on the f-file, but is also preparing to transfer his bishop to b6 or a5.
16.♘eg1
White plays originally, of course, but somehow ponderously and unnaturally...
16...♘e7 17.♘g5 ♖f6 18.♔f1

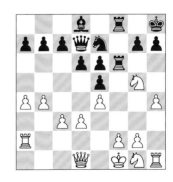

To be honest, I still don't understand why this move is needed. And Black acts very consistently.

18...c5! 19.bxc5 dxc5 20.♞5f3 ♞c6 21.♖d2 ♗a5 22.♛b3 a6

Black has 'set to work' all his pieces and has firmly seized the initiative. His plan is to create a passed pawn on the queenside.

23.♖d1 h6 24.h5 ♚h7

Perfectly played, Karpov-style! White is deprived of counterplay and is sinking deeper and deeper into time-trouble, while Black calmly improves the position of his king and invites his opponent to show his hand.

25.♛c4 Here the queen is subject to the ...b7-b5 advance, with tempo. But suggesting moves for White here is a thankless task.

25...♛d6 26.♞e2 ♖b8 27.♖b1 ♗c7! The bishop has done its job and is giving way to the knight – White is unable to prevent the advance ...b7-b5. His pieces are scattered across the board, whereas Black's forces interact perfectly.

28.♖h3 ♞a5 29.♛a2 b5 30.axb5 axb5 31.♖d1 b4 32.cxb4 cxb4 33.d4

Trying to muddy the waters, but with several clear moves Karjakin neutralizes his opponent's play and achieves a decisive advantage.

33...b3 34.♛b1 ♛b6! 35.dxe5 ♖f7

Black has sacrificed a pawn, but his passed b-pawn will cost his opponent at least a piece.

36.g4 b2 37.g5 ♚h8 38.gxh6 gxh6 39.♞ed4 ♞c6

39...♞c4 was also very strong. White's

The festively illuminated façade of the Central Chess Club on Gogolevsky Boulevard, a spark of light in grim times.

threats on the kingside are easily repulsed.

40.♞xc6 ♛xc6 41.♞h4 ♛c4+ 42.♖hd3 ♖b3 43.♞g6+ ♚g7 44.♚g1 ♖xd3 45.♖xd3 ♛c1+

White resigned in view of 46.♖d1 ♛g5+ 47.♚f1 ♛xh5, and the knight is lost.

The 2018 World Rapid Champion Daniil Dubov started with a beautiful victory over 18-year-old GM Andrey Esipenko. In the middlegame, Daniil sacrificed a queen for a rook and knight and pushed his passed pawn to the d7-square. Andrey had to send his queen to fight the pawn, and the queen, as you know, is a useless blocker.

Daniil Dubov
Andrey Esipenko
Moscow 2020 (1)

position after 24...♖e5

25.♛xc5!

White also has an advantage after the simple 25.♞xd7 ♞xd7 26.♛xa4 ♖xe2 27.♗xb7, but the queen sacrifice leads to a technically winning position.

25...♖xc5 26.♞xd7 ♛g5 27.♞xf8 ♚xf8

Black had an interesting tactical resource: 27...♖c8!?, with the idea of 28.♞d7 ♛xb5 29.♗h3 ♛c6+ 30.e4 ♛xe4+ 31.♗g2 ♛e3, getting some counterplay. But as GM A. Tukhaev pointed out on the ChessPro website, White has 28.♖d5!, with the main variation 28...♛g4 29.h3! ♛xg3 30.♞d7, and the knight breaks free.

28.d7 ♛d8 29.♖xf2 ♖c7 30.♗h3 g6 31.♖f6

The human solution: White blocks the f7-pawn so it cannot block the bishop's diagonal. The computer alternative is 31.♗e6 ♚e7 32.b6! ♖c5 33.♗xf7, etc.

31...♚g8 32.♖fd6 ♖c2 33.♖6d2 ♖c7 34.♖d3 f5 35.b6 ♖c2 36.♖e3

The rook has made its way to the Black camp, and Esipenko admitted defeat.

The rating favourite of the championship, and the later champion, also celebrated victory in the first round and selected this game to annotate after he had claimed the title.

NOTES BY
Ian Nepomniachtchi

Ian Nepomniachtchi
Maxim Matlakov
Moscow 2020 (1)
Queen's Gambit Declined, Exchange Variation

1.d4 ♘f6 2.c4 e6 3.♘c3 d5 4.cxd5 exd5 5.♗g5 ♗b4

Maxim uses a comparatively rare hybrid of the Queen's Gambit and the Ragozin Defence, whose main advocate is Alexander Riazantsev. Dubov, Motylev and Matlakov himself have also played this, mainly in rapid games.

6.e3 h6 7.♗h4 g5 8.♗g3 ♘e4

Black's basic idea is to somehow gain the advantage of the bishop pair. The measured, Carlsbad-like course of the game is quickly disrupted, and the customary guidelines are not fully effective. For example, the minority attack, familiar since our childhood, is not something that White can count on. ☺

9.♘ge2 h5 10.h4

One of the differences with the Ragozin Defence is the possibility of developing the knight to e2, from where it controls squares c3 and g3. White manages without the move f3, and the important dark squares in the centre and on the kingside remain under his control.

10...♘xg3 11.♘xg3 gxh4 12.♘xh5 ♕g5

Black's achievements may seem dubious – the h-pawn will become a target, the knight on h5 may return to f4. He has also left his queenside

undeveloped. Yet it is not at all easy to demonstrate an advantage for White. Both the text-move and 12...c6, after which Black carefully completes his development, promise a full-scale battle.

13.♕a4+ By forcing Black to place his knight on c6, White plans to exploit the vulnerability of the d5-pawn.

13...♘c6 14.♘f4

14...♖h6! Vertically developing a rook is something that I have always liked, and in this case it is also the strongest move. After 14...♗d7 15.♕b5 ♘xd4 16.♕xb7 ♖d8 17.0-0-0 ♗xc3 18.bxc3 ♘e6 19.♘xd5 White is a sound pawn to the good.

15.♕b5 ♗f5!?

A new move. 15...♗d6 16.g3 a6 17.♕e2 hxg3 18.♕h5 gave White an edge in Amico-Esposito, correspondence game 2018.

16.♘fxd5

'Something has to be captured – now is the time!' Black does not try to defend his numerous weaknesses and plays for activity. Taking with the queen on b7 is suicidal, and the capture 16.♕xd5 does not look too

good either: 16...♖d8 17.♕b5 a6 18.♕e2 ♔d7 (yes, this can also be played) 19.0-0-0 ♔c8.

16...a6 17.♕a4 ♗d6 18.0-0-0

18...♔f8

Here I concluded that I was not worse (18....0-0-0 won't work in view of 19.♗xa6). Since Maxim had played very quickly so far, and I unfortunately didn't remember the accurate response to 15...♗f5, it only remained for me to await new surprises. Trying to assess the outcome of the opening is a thankless task. White has an extra pawn, harmoniously placed pieces, and a stable centre. Black, at first sight, has only the two bishops and boundless confidence, but his position in fact contains a great reserve of potential energy, which will become kinetic as soon as the b-pawn is able to advance. The situation is probably one of the proverbial dynamic balance, but in order to maintain it, Black will have to play more accurately than his opponent.

19.f4 In the Soviet Union, *Strike first, Freddy!* was a popular Danish comedy, parodying spy thrillers like the James Bond films. Why do I mention this? Simply because I decided that in this type of position, you have to strike first. The move is undoubtedly not the best, but Black now faces a choice after practically every move. The outwardly calmer 19.♗e2 did not guarantee any calm: 19...♖e8 20.♗f3 b5 21.♕xa6 ♘b4 22.♘xb4 ♗xb4 23.♕a7 h3 (an important idea: Black wants to leave the bishop on f3 undefended; in such a sharp position the stakes are high!) 24.gxh3 ♖xe3 25.fxe3 ♕xe3+ 26.♖d2 ♕xf3, with an unclear position and – in the event of accurate play by both sides – drawing tendencies.

19...♕g6

To me this seemed to be the obvious and virtually only move. If White advances his e-pawn, his king will use the respite to hide on b1 or a1, so White won't have to worry about the position being opened. Nevertheless, Maxim spent more than half an hour here, losing his entire opening time-advantage.

20.♗e2

20...♖e8

'Shut the door, they're coming through the window!' With f4, White had supposedly driven the queen from the e3-square, but 20...♕e6 would have forced him back to the negotiating table. 21.g4 hxg3 22.♖xh6 ♕xh6 23.♗f3 seemed very thematic to me, but after 23...♕h2 24.♖d2 ♕h4 (24...♕g1+? 25.♕d1, and the endgame is very bad for Black) 25.♖d1 ♕h2 White has to agree to repetition.

21.♗f3 b5 The afore-mentioned

Maxim Matlakov has his temperature measured. Anti-corona precautions were strict and manifold all through the Super Final.

resource 21...h3 would have forced White to play accurately:
– 22.g4 ♗xg4 23.♗xg4 (23.♖dg1 ♗xf3 24.♖xg6 fxg6 25.♖h2 is terribly interesting, but from a human point of view more terrible than interesting) 23...♕xg4 24.♖dg1 ♕f3 25.♖f1 ♕g3 26.♖fg1, with repetition.
– The simple-minded 22.gxh3

'Insanity is doing the same thing over and over again and expecting different results'

loses: 22...♘b4 23.♖hg1 ♕e6 24.e4 ♘xd5 25.♘xd5 ♗xe4 26.♖de1 b5! (preventing ♖g8+ and other tricks) 27.♕b3 ♕f5 28.♖xe4 ♖xe4 29.♕c2 ♖g6 (again preventing the motif ♖g8+ and ♘f6) 30.♖d1 (30.♖xg6 ♖e1+) 30...♖ge6 31.♗xe4 ♖xe4, and White can only hope for a miracle.

22.♕xa6

22...♘b8?

Maxim's first significant error. It is amusing that on the previous move, instead of 21... b5, 21...♘b8 was not at all bad.
Simplifying the position was more logical and stronger: 22...♘e7 23.♘xe7 (23.g4!? 'Have I already told you what insanity is? Insanity is doing the same thing over and over again and expecting different results. This is insanity.' *Far Cry* (and Albert Einstein, for that matter – ed).
For some reason, I very much believed in the many possibilities of the move g4 during the game, but it

would appear that it almost always leads to a draw. Here is an example: 23...♗xg4 24.♖dg1 ♗xf3 25.♖xg6 ♖xg6 26.♖xh4 ♖g1+ 27.♔d2 ♖g2+ 28.♔c1) 23...♖xe7. In the complications, Black seems to be holding everything together, although the position is more suitable for analysis than for playing.

23.♕b7 c6 24.♘c7

The only move, but more than adequate.

24...♖c8

24...♖xe3 won't work: 25.♕xb8+ ♔g7 26.♘e8+ ♖xe8 27.♕xe8 ♗xf4+ 28.♖d2 ♕g5 29.♕e1 ♖e6 30.♘e2, and White can set about converting his advantage.

25.e4!

25.♘a8 ♖e8 26.♘c7 would have brought the players slightly closer to the time-control on move 40.

25.♗e4 ♗xc7? 26.g4! was a nice trap, but alas, capturing the knight with the bishop is not forced: 25...♖xc7, 25...♕f6 and even 25...♖d8 leads to unclear play.

25...♗xc7 26.exf5 ♕xf5 27.♗e4 ♕d7 28.♔b1 ♗xf4 29.♕b6

Here it was possible to swap the queens, eyeing the extra pawn in the endgame: 29.♕xd7 ♘xd7 30.d5 ♘c5 31.♗f5 ♖b8 32.dxc6 ♖xc6 33.♖xh4 ♗e5, but this was somehow faint-hearted.

29...♕d6?

So bad that it was even good. I had not expected this move at all, and I completely forgot that I was planning to advance d4-d5 at the first opportunity.

30.♖hf1?!

30.d5 cxd5 31.♕xb5, and White has either an extra pawn, a winning position, or both: 31...d4 (31...♖xc3 32.bxc3 ♕c7 33.♕xd5 ♖d6 34.♕h5, winning) 32.♕f5 ♖e8 33.♖hf1 ♖f6 34.♕h5 ♖h6 35.♕f3, and wins.

30...♘d7 31.♕a6 ♖e8 32.♗c2 ♘f6 Black has coordinated his forces, and the question of immediate capitulation has been removed from the agenda.

33.a3?

33.d5 cxd5 34.♕xb5 ♖b8 35.♕a5 ♗e5 36.b3 would have retained memories of the decisive advantage, but the position is now one in which both sides have play.

33...♕c7?

Maxim was the first player to end up in time-trouble, and this undoubtedly influenced the outcome of the game. For example, at this point, healthy optimism would have enabled him to equalize completely: 33...♕g4! 34.♖de1 ♘e3 35.♖f3 ♕xd4 36.♗b3 ♖f6.

34.d5?

An emotional decision. The queen on a6 has no moves, and after ...♖b8 and ...♘d5 the threat of it getting trapped

becomes real, although in the event of the accurate 34.♖f3 ♖b8 35.♘e2 ♘d5 36.♘xf4 ♘xf4, the rook on h6 will be temporarily undefended, and White develops an irresistible attack: 37.♗b3 ♔g7 38.♖df1 c5 39.♕xh6+ ♔xh6 40.♖xf4, winning.

34...♘xd5 35.♘xd5 cxd5 36.♕xb5 ♖b6 37.♕xd5

37...♕c3

After the logical 37...♗e5 38.b4 ♗f6 39.♗b3, the extra pawn does not play any role, and the white and black monarchs feel equally uncomfortable.

38.b4

38...♖f6??

With this move, literally played in the last second, Maxim commits a nightmarish blunder. The obvious (and only) move 38...♖d6 would have maintained equality. For example, 39.♖d3 ♖e1+ 40.♖xe1 ♕xe1+ 41.♖d1 ♕c3 42.♕b3 ♖xd1+ 43.♗xd1 ♕xb3+ 44.♗xb3 ♔e7. After placing his bishop on e1 Black easily makes a draw.

39.♖xf4 Black resigned.

This successful start set the tone for my subsequent performance.

■ ■ ■

Karjakin in the lead

After three rounds, Sergey Karjakin, having won again as Black, became the sole leader.

Nikita Vitiugov
Sergey Karjakin
Moscow 2020 (3)

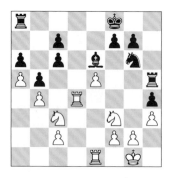

position after 20...♔f8

In this notorious Berlin endgame, Nikita Vitiugov, who is famous for his deep theoretical ideas, applied a new plan: he moved the outside pawn to a5 and transferred the queen's rook to the centre via a4. Karjakin carried out a similar regrouping on the

Karjakin was not sure of the defensibility of his fortress and was constantly looking for dynamic ways to complicate things

kingside: his pawn came to h4, and his rook to h5. Vitiugov's position looked very promising, especially after he secured the enemy queenside pawns. Karjakin admitted afterwards that he was not sure of the defensibility of his fortress at that point, and was constantly looking for dynamic ways to complicate the struggle.

21.♖dd1?!
The St. Petersburg grandmaster could

Mikhail Antipov had to leave the Super Final after Round 6 after he had tested positive for Covid-19. According to the rules the results in his games stood.

sacrifice a pawn for a powerful blockading knight on c5 and a strong initiative: 21.♘e4!? ♘xe5 22.♘xe5 ♖xe5 23.♖ed1 (or 23.f4!?). Also interesting is 21.♖e3!?, followed by 22.♘e4.
21...♖e8 22.♘d4
Now 22.♘e4 is not so strong anymore due to 22...♘xe5 23.♘xe5 ♖xe5 24.♘c5 ♖xe1+ 25.♖xe1 ♗c8, and Black has managed to bring the rook into play and defended the a6-pawn with the bishop.

Fighting for the elusive initiative, Vitiugov overestimates his chances. He should have gone for 24.♘d5 ♖hxe5 25.♖xe5 ♘xe5 26.bxc5 ♖c6 27.♘b4 ♖xc5 28.♘xa6 ♖xc2 29.♖d5.
24...♖e8
Objectively stronger was 24...♔e7 25.♖ed1 ♖c6!, but here it is more difficult for Black to keep the situation under control, since White's pieces are very active.
25.♖xe8+ ♔xe8 26.♘d5 ♔d7

22...c5! It is important for Black to 'seal' the hole on c5. In favour of White is 22...♘xe5 23.♘xe6+ ♖xe6 24.♘e4 or 22...♖xe5 23.♖xe5 ♘xe5 24.♘e4 ♗c8 25.♘c5+.
23.♘xe6+ ♖xe6 24.♖d8+?!

27.f4?! A serious inaccuracy. Better was 27.♖d1, after which Black would have to find the subtle manoeuvre 27...♖h6! 28.f4 ♘e7.
27...c6 28.♘b6 ♔e7 29.♘c8+ ♔e6 30.♘d6?

Vitiugov bets on his outside passed pawn, allowing his opponent to sharply activate his king and obtain a whole 'gang' of pawns aiming to queen. It was necessary to switch to another pawn: 30.♘a7! ♞xf4 31.♘xc6 ♖g5 32.♔h1!?, with chances of a draw. **30...♞xf4 31.♘e4 cxb4 32.♘c5+ ♔d5 33.♘xa6 c5 34.♖d1+ ♔c4 35.♘c7**

35...♞e6! 36.♘d5 ♞d4 37.♘b6+ ♔c3 38.a6 ♔xc2 39.a7 ♖h8 Black is ready to give up his rook for the passed pawn, since his own pawns are unstoppable. **40.♖f1 b3 41.♖f2+ ♔d3 42.♘d7 ♖a8** White resigned.

The next day, Ian Nepomniachtchi also reached the plus-two mark, defeating Mikhail Antipov with black.

Mikhail Antipov
Ian Nepomniachtchi
Moscow 2020 (4)

position after 21.♖b1

Ian had played his favourite Najdorf. At first, the struggle developed quite calmly, but as soon as knots had to be cut, Nepomniachtchi showed his class. Suddenly clouds were hanging over the white king; in order not to fall under a devastating attack, Antipov sacrificed an exchange, but he could only resist for a short while. **21...♗e2**

22.♕c6?
He could have held with 22.♕a7! ♖d2 23.♖fe1 ♕g5 24.♕e3 or 24.♕e7!?.
22...♖d2 23.♖fe1 ♕g5!
24...♗f3 is threatened, with checkmate on the light squares. Antipov could hardly have missed such a simple threat. Perhaps he had counted on 24.♕xd6 ♗f3 25.♕xf8+! ♔xf8 26.♖b8+, and had missed the intermediate sacrifice 24...♖xd5! 25.♕xd5, and only now 25...♗f3 26.g3 ♕h5, with inevitable checkmate.

24.♖xe2
The most persistent. The position after 24.♘e3 ♗f3 25.♕c4 h5 resembles a football penalty: 24.♕d7 ♗f3 25.♕h3 ♗xe4! 26.♖xe4 ♖xd5.
24...♖xe2 25.♕xd6 ♖e8 26.♕d7 ♖e6 27.g3 ♕h5 28.♔g2
The attempt to create an attack on the king with 28.♕d8+ ♔h7 29.♘e7 runs into 29...♖xe7 30.♕xe7 ♕f3 31.♖f1 ♖xe4, with the extremely unpleasant threat of ...h5-h4.
28...♔h7 29.♕d8 ♕g4 30.♖b4 ♖g6 The brutal 31...♕xg3+ is threatening, and there is no defence against it. White resigned.

Nepo and Karjakin set the pace
At this point, it had become clear that Nepomniachtchi and Karjakin were in excellent form and that the main struggle for the championship would probably unfold between them. And so it happened, but with a serious 'correction' by Dubov that really played out only in the second half of the tournament. In the early rounds the Muscovite was playing too riskily.

The sixth round turned out to be one of the most combative. Ian Nepomniachtchi beat the lowest-rated participant in this stellar company, Alexei Goganov, as Black. Ian's opening preparation turned out to be deeper, he seized the initiative and soon won the exchange. Goganov's attempts to create counterplay on the kingside came to nothing and after reaching the time control, the grandmaster from St. Petersburg resigned.

However, Nepomniachtchi did not become the sole leader, because Sergey Karjakin caught up with him after beating Maxim Matlakov as White. Sergey Karjakin: 'The game turned out to be very difficult. Despite the fact that I came well-prepared, Maxim managed to surprise me with a queen sacrifice for a rook and bishop. I thought for a long time and decided to play the most principled continuation. Objectively, Black should hold, but in a practical game it was not so easy, and at some point Matlakov played an inaccurate move. I think I did a pretty good job in the conversion phase. Of course, my opponent's final blunder made my task easier, but even without this, White's position should be winning.'

Sergey Karjakin
Maxim Matlakov
Moscow 2020 (6)
Catalan Opening

1.d4 ♘f6 2.c4 e6 3.♘f3 d5 4.g3 ♗b4+ 5.♗d2 a5 6.♗g2 0-0 7.♕c2 c5 8.cxd5 cxd4 9.♘xd4 ♕b6 10.e3 exd5 11.0-0 ♘c6 12.♘xc6 bxc6 13.♖c1 ♗e6

This is how the game Ding Liren-Giri, Yekaterinburg 2020, developed: 13...♖b8 14.♗xb4 ♕xb4 15.b3 h5 16.♘c3 h4 17.♘e2 ♗d7 18.♘f4 hxg3 19.hxg3 ♖fc8 20.♗f3 a4 21.bxa4 ♖a8 22.♘d3 ♕xa4 23.♕xa4 ♖xa4 24.♘c5, and Black was saved only by a miracle.

14.♕xc6!? In the game Esipenko-Riazantsev, Tallinn 2019, White played the modest 14.♘c3, but Karjakin accepts the challenge.
14...♗xd2 15.♕xb6 ♗xc1 16.♕d4 ♖fb8 17.b3 ♖b4 18.♕d3
In case of 18.♕c3 (and even more so 18.♕e5?) 18...♖c8!, the advantage is on Black's side.
18...♗b2

19.a3!
An important tactical nuance on which White's play is based.

Mikhail Antipov tested positive for Covid-19 and had to drop out of the competition

19...♗xa1 20.axb4 axb4 21.h3 h6?! 22.f4! ♖c8 23.♘d2 ♖c1+ 24.♘f1 ♗c3?!
More stubborn is 24...♖c5, not giving up the central pawn without a fight.
25.f5 ♗d7 26.♗xd5 ♗e5 27.g4 ♖c3 28.♕a6!
Stronger than 28.♕d1 ♗b5!.
28...♘xd5 29.♕a8+ ♗c8 30.♕xd5 ♗f6 31.♘d2 ♖c1+ 32.♔h2 ♖d1 33.♔g3 ♗c3 34.♕d8+ ♔h7 35.♕xc8 ♖xd2 36.♕e8 f6 37.h4 ♖d1 38.♔g2 ♖d2+ 39.♔f3 ♖d5 More tenacious was 39...♖d1. Now, thanks to the 'hanging' rook on d5, White goes for a decisive breakthrough.

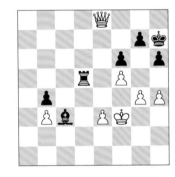

40.♕g6+ ♔h8 41.g5! hxg5 42.hxg5 fxg5 43.f6 g4+ 44.♕xg4
And in view of 44...♗xf6 45.♕h3+ ♔g8 46.♕e6+, Black resigned.

After six rounds, Sergey Karjakin and Ian Nepomniachtchi had scored 4½ points each and were one point ahead of Vladislav Artemiev and Vladimir Fedoseev. Before the rest day, the participants took a Covid test again. Mikhail Antipov tested positive, and unfortunately had to drop out of the competition. Then, right after the break, the encounter between the leaders took place.

NOTES BY
Anish Giri

Ian Nepomniachtchi
Sergey Karjakin
Moscow 2020 (7)
Nimzo-Indian Defence, Kmoch Variation

Always a principled duel between these two!
1.d4 ♘f6 2.c4 e6 3.♘c3 ♗b4 4.f3

Ian Nepomniachtchi is expanding his repertoire a lot these days, and here he chooses a principled line that Sergey Karjakin couldn't possibly have expected.
4...d5 5.a3 ♗e7 One of the trendy systems against the 4.f3 Nimzo, that Sergey had played before.
6.e4 dxe4 7.fxe4 c5

This is the point: Black has allowed White to build an impressive pawn centre, but now he starts undermining it.
8.d5 exd5 9.exd5 0-0 10.♗e2
The correct move order, which my wife [Sopiko Guramishvili – ed.] recommended in her f3 Nimzo series for chess24.com when it was still a new move. The idea is to delay ♘f3

and prevent getting pinned by ...♗g4 too early in some lines.

10...♖e8 11.♘f3 ♗g4 12.0-0 ♘bd7 13.d6 So far, this has all been played in quite a few high-level games. **13...♗f8 14.h3 ♗h5**

15.♗f4!? A new idea. Previously, White had always tried 15.♘b5, as in Caruana-Alekseenko in the Candidates, and in Vidit Gujrathi-Aronian and Vidit Gujrathi-Karjakin in online events, all of them in 2020.

15...♕b6 Connecting the rooks – an excellent reaction.

16.b3!? This looks timid, but White is defending the b-pawn and wants to deploy the rook via a2.

16...♖ad8 Very natural, but the alternatives, e.g. 16...♖e6 and 16...♘e4, should be investigated as well.

17.♖a2! h6 A decent waiting move.

18.a4 Pushing the flank soldier. The idea now is that the a5-push becomes an option at an opportune moment. This works out beautifully.

18...♗xf3? Black decides to finally start some concrete action, but it doesn't work. There were many alternatives, from the concrete 18...♘e4 to useful waiting moves like 18...a6!?.

In the encounter between the leaders halfway through, Ian Nepomniachtchi defeated Sergey Karjakin in a powerful game.

19.♗xf3 ♘e5 20.♘b5!
The knight is sitting perfectly here, since ...a6 can be met by a5!, when the queen on b6 is trapped.

20...♗xd6?
Trying to justify the previous sequence, but this will lose by force. Instead, 20...♘xf3+ 21.♕xf3 ♕c6 would have kept the game going, although the position is not good for Black at this point: 22.♘c7 ♖e4 23.♘d5 ♖e6. Black has everything protected, but now 24.♗xh6!? is a promising blow, as is the silent 24.♖e2!, upping the ante.

21.a5! This push comes in handy.
21...♕a6 22.♖d2

Black will lose material due to the pin.
22...♘xf3+ 23.♖xf3 ♘e4 Black gets a rook for two pieces, but White is so well coordinated that the game has already been decided at this point.
24.♘xd6 ♘xd2 25.♕xd2 ♖e6 26.♖d3

White has perfect central control and his huge firepower is poised to shift to the kingside.

26...b6 27.♘f5 ♖xd3 28.♕xd3

Now Black has to reckon with the threat of ♕g3.

28...♕b7

Preparing to meet 29.♕g3 with 29...♖g6.

29.♕d5!

A powerful move. White bullies Black's queen, using the fact that a queen exchange creates a very dangerous passed d-pawn.

29...♕xd5

The endgame is lost, since the d-pawn will queen, but there were no alternatives. 29...♕c8 would have lost to 30.♗e5!, when there is no comfortable way to protect the g7-pawn.

30.cxd5 ♖e1+ 31.♔f2 ♖d1 32.♔e2!

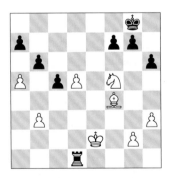

Kicking the rook away from the d-file using the ...♖xd5? ♘e7+ tactic.
Black resigned.
A powerful game by Nepo, starting with great prep and finishing with a top-notch conversion.

■ ■ ■

Ambitious and energetic

And so, was the fight for first place over? No, Karjakin begged to differ! In Round 8, he played as White against one of his biggest rivals, Peter Svidler (chess fans will probably never forget their epic final at the 2015 World Cup in Baku). In a Najdorf, Black got a rather unpleasant position from the opening, but then, exploiting White's inaccuracy, Svidler successfully opened the position and practically equalized. But he had spent a lot of time and got into severe time-trouble. The position, with queens and rooks and open kings, remained extremely sharp, and on the 34th

Dubov and Riazantsev had prepared a 'bomb' against a weapon that Nepomniachtchi regularly uses

move Black made a blunder and found himself under a mating attack.

On the same day, Ian Nepomniachtchi did not play very well as White against Vladimir Fedoseev and found himself a pawn down. However, it was not easy for Black to convert it, since there was little material left, and White's bishops controlled the entire board. Nepomniachtchi showed tenacity in defence and saved half a point. But his lead over Karjakin was now also only half a point.

Nepomniachtchi did not remain the sole leader for long – after Round 9, Karjakin restored the status quo. On this day, Ian played black against Daniil Dubov, an ambitious and energetic player with his own pronounced creative style. Dubov's collaboration with Alexander Riazantsev, a strong player (Russian champion in 2016), an experienced trainer and an authoritative theorist,

has been very fruitful. Together they had prepared a 'bomb' against a weapon that Nepomniachtchi regularly uses.

Daniil Dubov
Ian Nepomniachtchi
Moscow 2020 (9)
Grünfeld Defence, Exchange Variation

1.d4 ♘f6 2.c4 g6 3.♘c3 d5 4.cxd5 ♘xd5 5.e4 ♘xc3 6.bxc3 ♗g7 7.♗b5+

Daniil Dubov had never played like this before, but these days it doesn't really matter. More importantly, Ian Nepomniachtchi did have experience with this line and it was more or less clear what he was guided by.

7...c6 8.♗a4 b5 9.♗b3 a5 10.♘f3 0-0 11.0-0 a4 12.♗c2 c5 13.♖b1 ♘c6

14.d5

In the game Nakamura-Nepomniachtchi, Paris 2019 (Grand Chess Tour, blitz), Black got excellent counterplay after 14.♗e3 cxd4 15.cxd4 ♗g4 16.♖xb5 ♗xf3 17.gxf3 ♗xd4 18.♖d5 ♗xe3 19.♖xd8 ♖fxd8 20.♕e2 ♗f4. Formally, the move in the game is a novelty, but since this is the first line of the computer, it is clear that it was not a surprise.

14...♞e5 15.♞xe5 ♝xe5 16.♝h6

16...♝a6

Ian had been playing very fast so far, so this exchange sacrifice was obviously brought from home.

In case of 16...♜e8?! 17.♛e1! (so that 17...♛a5 can be answered with 18.♝d2) White plays f2-f4 and obtains a great attacking position.

17.♝xf8 ♚xf8 18.f4 ♝xc3 19.♜f3

19...♛a5?!

And Ian pondered this dubious decision for about 20 minutes. Later he explained what had happened: 'Much knowledge – many sorrows! The night before the game I had repeated the variation that appeared on the board, but as I was sitting there I could not remember exactly how to continue. I mixed things up and instead of reaching an equal position I ended up in a hopeless one.'

So what should he have played? The first option that suggests itself is 19...♝d4+ 20.♚h1 ♚g8 21.♛e1 ♜b8, with counterplay on the queenside, while White still cannot push

e4-e5 as it would lose the d5-pawn. Stockfish's recommendation is also interesting: 19...b4!? 20.♝xa4 (20.e5? ♝d4+ 21.♚h1 ♛xd5) 20...♝c8 21.h3 ♛a5 22.♝c6 ♜a6, after which Black gets to the a2-pawn.

20.e5

20...♚g8?

The second part of the mix-up. Here the counterattack on the d5-pawn by 20...♝d4+ 21.♚h1 ♝b7 does not work: 22.♜h3 ♚g7 23.f5! ♝xe5 24.♜xh7+! ♚xh7 25.fxg6+ ♚g8 26.♛f3, with a devastating attack. But there was still time to strengthen the g6- and h7-squares: 20...♚g7!

21.♜h3 ♝d4+ 22.♚h1 ♜h8!?, and it is much more difficult for White to develop an attack.

21.♚h1!?

A sign of high chess culture: it is useful to secure your own king before starting an assault. But the 'uncultured' computer immediately gets into the fight: 21.e6 fxe6 22.♜g3! ♝g7 23.♛g4, and the attack cannot be stopped.

21...♜d8 A little respite doesn't really help Black. For example, counterplay with 21...b4 proves insufficient: 22.e6 b3 (22...f5 23.d6) 23.exf7+ ♚xf7 24.axb3 a3,

With his creative style Daniil Dubov continues to be popular. Together with his trainer Alexander Riazantsev he had prepared 'a bomb' that took Ian Nepomniachtchi by surprise.

ANALYSIS DIAGRAM

and here, with a computer assessment of about +6, a combinational fireworks starts. Here is just one of many beautiful variations: 25.f5 a2 26.fxg6+ ♔e8 27.d6! axb1♕ 28.♗xb1 ♗d4 29.g7 ♗xg7 30.♖e3 ♗f6 31.dxe7 ♗xe7 32.♕h5+, with a win.

22.e6! fxe6

23.♗xg6!
Very impressive, although typical of a number of variations of the Grünfeld Defence, in which the black king has to take care of his own safety while his colleagues are busy with other problems on the opposite flank.

23...hxg6 24.♕c2 ♗g7

25.♖g3!
The offensive would slow down

after 25.♕xg6 ♕d2 26.♖g3 ♕d4, although, of course, here too after 27.♕xe6+ ♔f8 28.♕xa6 Black has nothing to be happy about.

25...g5 26.♕g6 ♕d2 27.♖xg5 ♕c3 28.♕xe6+ ♔f8

29.♖e1!
Dubov perfectly feels the initiative and again and again finds the clearest decisions. It was tempting to take the bishop, 29.♕xa6, but after 29...b4 30.♕e6 ♖d6 Black has built some sort of a defence.

29...♕xe1+ 30.♕xe1 ♗f6 31.♕h4!
The last move that deserves to be noted. Using the rook as a shield, the queen penetrates the opponent's back rank and the fight ends. The possible loss of an exchange does not bother White at all – in return he will get strong passed pawns.

31...♖d6
31...♗xg5 32.♕h8+ ♔f7 33.♕xd8 is hopeless for Black.

32.♕h7

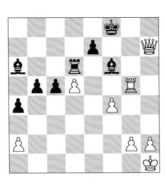

32...♔e8 In case of 32...♗xg5 33.fxg5 ♖xd5 34.h4 the white pawns are unstoppable.

33.♕g8+
Also good was 33.♖g8+ ♔d7 34.♖a8.

33...♔d7 34.♕a8 ♗xg5 35.fxg5 c4 36.h4 b4 37.♕a7+ ♔e8 38.♕b8+ ♔f7 39.♕xb4 ♖xd5 40.♕xa4 Black resigned.

In that same round, Karjakin played Black against Fedoseev, who used the variation against the Nimzo-Indian (with 4.f3) that 'Nepo' had used to defeat Karjakin. This time Sergey opted for a slightly passive, but very solid position. Fedoseev got some pressure, but didn't achieve anything significant, and with accurate play Karjakin earned an important half point and caught up with Nepomniachtchi.

In the penultimate 10th round, both leaders played White and both won. Nepomniachtchi again demonstrated powerful home preparation to defeat Esipenko.

NOTES BY
Jan Timman

Ian Nepomniachtchi
Andrey Esipenko
Moscow 2020 (10)
Petroff Defence, Marshall Variation

1.e4 e5 2.♘f3 ♘f6 3.♘xe5 d6 4.♘f3 ♘xe4 5.d4 d5 6.♗d3 ♗d6 7.0-0 0-0 8.c4 c6 9.♘c3 ♘xc3 10.bxc3 dxc4 11.♗xc4

11...♗f5 11...♗g4 used to be the normal reply in this main line of the Petroff, but these days, the top players almost exclusively play the text.

12.♗g5 ♛a5 13.d5

This advance was first played by Kasimdzhanov. There are three alternatives: 13.♘h4, 13.♗d3 and 13.♖e1. Nakamura played the latter move twice against Aronian in the Lindores Abbey final.

13...♛c7

Earlier in the tournament, Esipenko had played 13...♛c5 against Karjakin. After 14.♗b3 cxd5 15.♗e3 ♛c7 16.♘xd5 ♗e6 Black was OK. There was little doubt that Nepomniachtchi had an improvement for White up his sleeve here.

14.♖e1 h6

15.♘h4 A new move with a specific purpose. In Kasimdzhanov-Lei Tingjie, Douglas 2019, White played 15.♗h4, after which Black can just about maintain the balance with 15...♗g4! 16.h3 ♗h5.

15...♗h7 16.♗xh6!

The point of the previous move. The bishop sac will yield White at least a draw. Nepomniachtchi played this at once, clearly showing that he had prepared it at home.

16...gxh6 17.♛g4+ ♚h8 18.♘f5 ♗xf5 19.♛xf5

With one round to go Ian Nepomniachtchi consolidated his lead – shared with Sergey Karjakin – as he got the better of Andrey Esipenko in an excellent game.

19...f6!

The best move. It looks as if Black is abandoning the light squares around his king, but the black queen will now be a force to be reckoned with in the defence.

The alternative 19...♗xh2+ was not really enough: after 20.♚h1 ♛f4 21.♛h3! ♘d7 22.♖ad1 ♘b6 23.♖d4 White wins back the piece with advantage.

20.♖ad1 cxd5 21.♖xd5 ♛xc4 22.♖xd6

For the first time, Nepomniachtchi thought for a few minutes here, probably to check some variations, since the alternative 22.♛g6 is not

really correct. That would have allowed Black to claim a draw at once with 22...♛xd5, if he had been that way inclined.

22...♛f7 23.h4

The white pieces are optimally placed, so White starts reinforcing his kingside. In addition, the text has a venomous point that will be revealed below.

23...♛h7

A safe continuation; but 23...a5 was a good alternative, intending to possibly develop the rook to a6. A possible continuation, then, is 24.♛f4 ♛g7 25.♖e3 ♘d7 26.♖g3 ♛h7 27.h5

NEW IN CHESS bestsellers

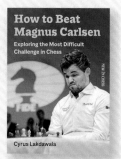

Exploring the Most Difficult Challenge in Chess
Cyrus Lakdawala

This fascinating book has a thematic structure, which, together with Lakdawala's uniquely accessible style, makes its lessons easy to digest. Sometimes even Magnus gets outplayed, sometimes he over-presses and goes over the cliff's edge, and sometimes he fails to find the correct plan. Lakdawala explains the how and the why.

Improve Your Ability to Spot Typical Mates
Vladimir Barsky

This is not just another book full of chess puzzles: it's a brilliantly organised course based on a Russian method that has proven to be effective. More often than you would expect, positions that look innocent at first sight, turn out to contain a mating pattern.

"A really important book, set out very clearly, extremely well organized." – *GM Daniel King*

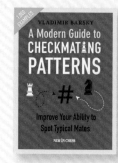

What You Can Learn From Tigran Petrosian's Extraordinary Defensive Skills
Alexey Bezgodov

When he had to defend, the 9th World Champion metamorphosed into a fearless adventurer who searched for counterplay at the cost of almost any concession. Former Russian Champion Alexey Bezgodov introduces 'The Other Petrosian' and teaches how to find creative solutions that will help you save lots of points.

A Practical Guide to Take Your Chess to the Next Level
Alex Dunne

Defeating 2000+ players will start feeling normal after working with this extended & improved edition of the bestselling classic. Based on real amateur games, Alex Dunne takes you by the hand and offers lots of practical, straightforward and effective advice. Slowly but surely, you will improve in all aspects of the game.

"Sprinkled throughout there are gems of advice." *Cecil Rosner, Winnipeg Free Press*

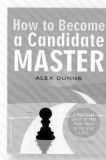

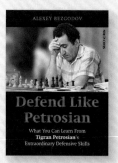

A Practical Guide to a Vital Skill in Chess
Merijn van Delft

"Excellent examples. Will have a major impact on your positional progress."
IM Gary Lane, Chess Moves Magazine

"A grandmaster-level skill explained in a comprehensible and readable fashion."
GM Matthew Sadler

"Masterfully discusses a vital topic, to bring your chess to the next level." – *GM Karsten Müller*

The Key to Better Calculation
Charles Hertan

New Edition of the award-winning classic: 50 extra pages!

"I love this book."
Elisabeth Vicary, USCF Online

"When the clock is ticking away, and you have too many viable candidate moves to choose from, remember Hertan's advice."
Steve Goldberg, ChessCafe

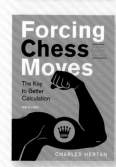

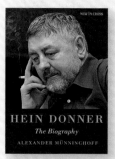

Hein Donner – The Biography
Alexander Münninghoff

"A fascinating insight into one of the most colourful characters in the chess world of that time and also an ideal complement to Donner's own writings in The King." – *Steve Giddins*

"Well-done by Münninghoff." – *Hans Ree*

"One of my five favourite chess books." – *Bent Larsen*

Ignore the Face Value of Your Pieces and Discover the Importance of Time, Space and Psychology in Chess   *Davorin Kuljasevic*

"Deserves a wide audience. One of the best books I have read this year." – *IM John Donaldson*

"A super piece of work, and an excellent take on a neglected area of the game." – *Ian Marks, Chess Schotland*

"Definitely has the potential to change the way a player thinks. A very good book." – *Sean Marsh, CHESS Monthly*

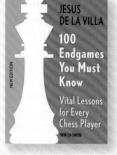

Vital Lessons for Every Chess Player
Jesus de la Villa

"If you've never read an endgame book before, this is the one you should start with."
GM Matthew Sadler, former British Champion

"If you really have no patience for endgames, at least read *100 Endgames You Must Know*."
Gary Walters Chess

Practical Techniques Everyone Should Know
Thomas Willemze

A no-nonsense guide with lots of fascinating examples and hundreds of instructive exercises.

"I can't think of another book that would be more helpful to the average player."
IM John Watson

"A truly superb learning guide for club players."
GM Matthew Sadler

available at your local (chess)bookseller or at www.newinchess.com

♖ae8 28.♖g6 ♖e1+ 29.♔h2 ♖e5!, and Black just about manages to save himself.

24.♕xh7+ ♔xh7 25.♖e7+

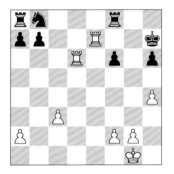

25...♔g6

An understandable move. One doesn't allow one's king to be cut off in the endgame. In this particular position, something special is going on, however: White can continue his attack despite the reduced material. This is why Black should have gone for the passive 25...♔g8. This looks a bit risky with White getting two rooks on the seventh rank, but this will yield him no more than a draw. A possible continuation is: 26.♖xb7 a5 27.♖d3 ♘c6 28.♖dd7 ♖fe8, and White has only perpetual check.

26.h5+! ♔g5

27.♖xb7

Amazingly enough, Nepomniachtchi had only used seven minutes so far, not counting the increments. He used four minutes for the text. Capturing the pawn seems obvious, but White had a stronger continuation in 27.♖d3!, continuing his attack. Black is forced to play 27...f5 (since 27...♘c6 will get him mated: 28.♖g3+ ♔f4

29.♖f3+ ♔g5 30.♖g7+, and mate next), but creating the hidey-hole on f6 cannot prevent Black's position from collapsing after 28.♖g3+ ♔f6 29.♖xb7 a5 30.♖g6+ ♔e5 31.♖xh6 – White already has three pawns for the piece, and his initiative is stronger than ever.

27...a5!

The only defence, again with the idea of developing the rook to a6. Black is going for a difficult but tenable rook ending.

28.g3 ♖a6!

Again, the young star finds the only move.

29.♖xb8 ♖xd6 30.♖xf8 ♖d2

A strange situation. White (temporarily) has two extra pawns, but the active positions of the black pieces make the win impossible.

31.a4 ♖a2 32.♔g2 f5

33.♖c8

The start of an ingenious plan that will severely test Black's defensive abilities. The endgame after 33.c4 ♖xa4 34.♔h3 ♖xc4 35.f4+ ♔xh5 36.♖xf5+ ♔g6 would be a theoretical draw.

33...♖xa4 34.♖c5 ♖a2 35.♔f3

This was the idea. At first sight, 36.g4 looks like a strong threat.

35...♔f6?

Panic. Esipenko still had seven minutes, but he played this immediately. Black had no reason to fear the advance of the g-pawn, because after 35...a4 36.g4 his king escapes to h4, where it is quite safe. After 36...♔h4 37.♖xf5 ♖c2 38.♖c5 a3 there is no way White can hold on to his pawn majority on the queenside, and a draw is inevitable.

36.♔e3 ♔g5 37.f3!

Now the situation has changed completely, the threat of 38.g4 being very strong in view of the fact that the white g-pawn will be solidly protected.

37...♔xh5

38.♔f4!

Another important finesse. White gets two decisive passed pawns.

38...♔g6 39.♖c6+ ♔g7 40.♔xf5 ♖f2 41.♖c7+ ♔f8 42.f4 ♖f3 43.g4 a4 44.c4 a3 45.♖a7 ♖c3 46.♔f6 ♔e8 47.c5 ♖c4 48.f5 ♖xg4 49.c6 ♔d8 50.♖xa3 ♔c7 51.♖h3 Black resigned.

■ ■ ■

Starting from a worse position

Sergey Karjakin's victory in the penultimate round against Vladislav Artemiev developed more dramatically. Vladislav often avoids principled opening lines, trying to start an independent game as early as possible. The main disadvantage of this approach when playing as Black is that it is often necessary to start that independent struggle in a worse position.

NOTES BY
Sergey Karjakin

Sergey Karjakin
Vladislav Artemiev
Moscow 2020 (10)
Ruy Lopez, Neo-Steinitz Variation

The first 'classical' tournament of the year (the last time I sat down at the board was in December 2019 at the Grand Prix in Jerusalem) unexpectedly turned out to be super-productive for me: +5 -2 =4! This made it difficult to choose what to comment on for the readers. I decided to focus on my game against Vladislav Artemiev. At this point, I was sharing first place with Ian Nepomniachtchi, and in order to fight for tournament victor I had to play for a win! Vlad is an interesting and original chess player, and facing him guarantees a tense and interesting struggle. Our game turned out to be convincing and quite clean on my part, which is rarely the case against opponents of such calibre as Artemiev.
1.e4! e5 2.♘f3 ♘c6 3.♗b5 a6 4.♗a4 d6 5.c3 ♗d7

Vlad had already played this variation, the Neo-Steinitz, several times in blitz on the Internet, including against Nakamura, and at the recent Russian Team Championship in Sochi against Najer, so I was ready for it.

6.0-0 g6 7.d4 ♘f6 8.♖e1 ♗g7 9.h3 0-0 10.♗c2 b5

Probably more accurate was 10...♖e8, preventing White's next move.

11.♗e3!?

A relatively fresh and rare continuation. White is still in no hurry to transfer the knight to g3. In some cases it can go to c5 after an exchange on e5. A blitz game between two modern classics saw 11.♘bd2 ♖e8 12.♘f1 ♘a5 13.b3 c5 14.d5 ♘h5 15.♗g5 ♕c7 16.♘g3 ♘f4 17.♕d2, and White had an advantage in Giri-Carlsen, Stavanger 2015 (½-½, 59).

11...exd4 A completely understandable decision to trade off White's 'Spanish bishop'.

After the standard way of playing 11...♖e8 12.♘bd2 ♘h5 13.♖c1!? (after this move d5 and c4 gain in strength in certain variations) 13...h6 14.♘f1 ♔h7 15.♕d2 White has simple and clear play in the centre.

12.cxd4! Unconvincing is 12.♘xd4 ♘e5!? 13.♘d2 c5 14.♘4f3 ♕c7, and Black had no problems in Vokhidov-Praggnanandhaa, Ahmedabad 2017 (0-1, 37).

12...♘b4 13.♘c3 ♘xc2 14.♕xc2
It now turns out that ...c7-c5, the standard play for such positions, is impossible, so we can talk about an advantage for White.

14...b4 15.♘e2 ♖e8 16.♘g3 h6?!
Preparing ...♘xe4, but creating an additional target for White's attack. It would have been better for the black king to leave this pawn in place: 16...a5 17.♗f4 (in order to play ♕d2) 17...♖a6 18.♕d2 ♕a8 19.e5 ♘d5 20.♗h6 ♗h8. This looks dangerous, but there is still a whole fight ahead.

17.♗d2! A key decision. This is the missing piece of the puzzle. It is very difficult, first of all psychologically, to make retreating moves. Now all White's pieces come into play.

17...a5 18.a3 bxa3
18...c5 runs into 19.♕c1! ♔h7 20.e5 ♘d5 21.♘e4, and White is winning.

19.♖xa3 a4 20.♕c1 ♔h7 21.e5!

21...♘g8
21...♘d5 is also met by 22.♖e4!, when

after 22...♖a6 23.♖h4 ♖c6 24.♕d1 Black is lost.

22.♖e4!

White's attack is progressing like clockwork! It's hard to come up with good advice for Black.

22...f6

Or 22...♗e6 23.♖h4 ♕e7 24.♖e3! ♗d5 25.♘e4, and White is winning.

23.♖h4 ♖f8

23...d5 24.♖c3 ♖a7 is refuted by 25.♗g5!, and after exchanges on f6 the knight will come to e5 with decisive effect.

24.exf6?

Oops, a mistake! I thought that I was already winning, but I had completely missed 24...♗xf6!.

Bringing in the only 'idler' in White's position, the knight on g3, would have led to a decisive advantage: 24.♘e4! fxe5 (24...f5 fails to 25.♗g5 ♕e8 26.♘f6+ and 24...g5 runs into 25.♘xf6+ ♗xf6 26.♘xg5+ ♗xg5 27.♗xg5, and wins) 25.dxe5 dxe5 26.♘eg5+ ♔h8 27.♖d3!.

ANALYSIS DIAGRAM

Black is absolutely helpless, e.g. 27...♕e8 28.♘xe5! ♗xe5 29.♖e3! ♗f5 30.♖xe5! ♖xe5 31.♗c3 ♖aa5 32.♗xa5

In the penultimate round Sergey Karjakin kept up with his rival Ian Nepomniachtchi as he convincingly beat the ever creative Vladislav Artemiev.

♖xa5 33.♕c3+ ♖e5 34.♕xe5+ ♕xe5 35.♘f7+ ♔g7 36.♘xe5, and White wins.

24...♗xf6!

I had only counted on the recapture with the queen or rook, when 25.♗g5 decides the issue in either case.

25.♖f4

Now I had to retreat with a heavy heart, because the planned 25.♗xh6 ♗xh4 26.♗xf8 runs up against 26...♗f6!. A cold shower! White needs to find 27.♘e4 ♕xf8 28.♕xc7 ♕d8 29.♕xd6, with equality.

An interesting attempt to continue the attack was 25.♖xh6+!? ♘xh6 26.♗xh6 ♗g7 27.♗g5!, when after

27...♕b8 (27...♗f6? 28.♘e4 ♗xg5 29.♘exg5+ ♔g7 30.d5, and Black is lost) 28.♗e7 ♖h6! 29.♘g5+ ♗xg5 30.♗xg5 ♕b7 31.♖c3 ♕d5 32.♖xc7 ♖f7 33.f3 White is still better. But I didn't want to sacrifice material in such a situation, even though objectively it was stronger than the game move.

25...♖c8?!

Vlad misses his chance: 25...♗g7! 26.♖xf8 ♕xf8 (26...♗xf8? 27.h4!) 27.♕xc7 ♘f6 and, despite being a pawn down, Black has quite good drawing chances. Perhaps this was the only moment in the game that he could have expected a positive result.

26.d5 c6 27.dxc6 ♗xc6

The alternative 27...♖xc6 doesn't bring any relief: 28.♕d1 ♗xb2 29.♖axa4 ♗g7 30.♖h4!, when White's rooks look very impressive!

28.♗c3

The engines emphatically advise playing 28.♕b1. While analysing this move, I came across a very beautiful variation, which I will gladly share: 28...♘e7 29.♘d4! ♗d7 30.♖af3 ♘d5 31.♖e4 ♕b6 32.♖xf6! ♖xf6 33.♖h4! a3 34.♘e4! ♕xb2 35.♘xf6+ ♔g7! 36.♕e4! (36.♗xh6+? only leads to a draw: 36...♔f7 37.♕e4 ♘xf6 38.♖f4 a2 39.♖xf6+ ♔xf6 40.♕f4+ ♗f5 41.♕xd6+ ♔f7 42.♕d5+ ♔f6, with a perpetual) 36...♕xd2.

ANALYSIS DIAGRAM

As a matter of fact, this is the position in which it all starts. White has only one move leading to victory,

viz. ... 37.♔h2!!. This idea reminded me very strongly of the famous game Khismatullin-Eljanov, 2015 European Championship in Jerusalem (see New In Chess 2015/3 – ed.), in which a similar manoeuvre of the white king brought him victory! 37...♘xf6 (37...a2 loses: 38.♕xd5 a1♕ 39.♕xd6! ♕aa2 40.♕e5 ♔f7 41.♘e4, and Black can resign) 38.♕e7+ ♔g8 39.♘e6! ♖h5 40.♕xd7 ♕c3 41.♖g4! g5 42.♘xg5! hxg5 43.♖xg5+ ♘g7 44.♖g3!, and White wins.

28...♗xf3 29.♖xf3 d5 30.♕d1

30...♗xc3 Black achieves little with 30...d4 31.♗b4 ♖e8 32.♖xa4.

31.♖fxc3 ♕b6 After 31...♖xc3 32.♖xc3 ♕d7 33.♕c2 ♖f7 White has 34.h4!, hinting at the weakness of the black king.

32.♕c2 ♖xc3 33.♖xc3 ♘e7 34.h4!

An already familiar idea. After this

modest move of the outside pawn, it finally becomes clear that Black cannot hold the position due to his numerous weaknesses and the open position of his king. More eloquent authors would write that 34.h4 was the straw that broke the camel's back.

34...♔g7 35.h5 g5

36.♖e3!

Not walking into the insidious trap 36.♖c7? ♖xf2!, when after 37.♕g6+! (37.♖xe7+ ♖f7+!) 37...♕xg6 38.hxg6 ♖xb2 39.♖xe7+ ♔xg6 40.♖e6+ ♔f7 41.♖a6 it's going to be a draw.

36...♖f7 37.♕e2

37...♘f5

Black could have put up more resistance with 37...♕c5, but it would not have changed the outcome: 38.♖e6 ♘g8 39.♖a6! ♕c1+ 40.♘f1 ♕f4 41.♕c2! ♕f5 42.♕xf5 ♖xf5 43.♘e3 ♖f7 44.♖xa4, etc.

38.♖e6 ♕d4 39.♖g6+

Also winning was 39.♘xf5+ ♖xf5 40.♕c2! ♕f4 41.g3 ♕f3 42.♖g6+ ♔h8 43.♖xh6+ ♔g7 44.♖a6.

39...♔f8 40.♘xf5 ♖xf5 41.♖xh6 ♖f6 42.♖h8+ ♔g7 43.♖e8 g4

Here I fully calculated the variation with mate to the king on h3.

This idea reminded me very strongly of the famous game Khismatullin-Eljanov, in which a similar manoeuvre of the white king brought him victory!

44.♕e7+ ♔h6 45.♖h8+ ♔g5
46.♖g8+ ♔h4 46...♔f5 loses to
47.♕d7+ ♖e6 48.♖g6. 47.g3+ ♔h3
48.♕e1 ♕d3 49.♖e8!

Black is defenceless against the threat
of ♖e2 and ♕f1 mate!
49...a3 50.♖e2 ♖xf2 51.♕xf2
Black resigned.

■ ■ ■

And this game from Round 10 essentially decided on the bronze medal.

Vladimir Fedoseev
Daniil Dubov
Moscow 2020 (10)

position after 16.♕e2

Once again, Daniil Dubov had played the opening very creatively: 1.e4

Vladimir Fedoseev's win in Round 10 threw Daniil Dubov out of the championship race and, as it turned out, secured third place for the grandmaster from St. Petersburg.

e5 2.♘f3 ♘c6 3.♗c4 d6 4.c3 f5!? At grandmaster level, this plan, it seems, was first applied by Ivan Sokolov in 2013, and in 2020 David Paravyan played this way several times on the Internet (where else?). Vladimir Fedoseev, apparently, was ready for it, as he played quite quickly and confidently.

Where to withdraw the queen to? 16...♕e6 is not good in view of 17.♕xe6 ♗xe6 18.♖e1 ♔d7 19.c4 d5 20.♘c3, but 16...♕g5 17.♘d2 ♖de8 18.♘e4 ♕g6

ANALYSIS DIAGRAM

gives White only a small initiative. For example, as Fedoseev pointed

out, 19.d5 is not dangerous for Black in view of 19...♘e5 20.♗xe5 ♗xb5 21.♕xb5 ♕xe4. Daniil, however, did not like it, and he tried something else.

16...♕g6? A mistake, as will become evident after White's fine 20th move.
17.♗xc6 ♗xc6 18.♕xe7 ♖de8
19.♕f7 ♖e2

Is 20.♕xg6 bad now? 20...♖xg2+, and in case of 20.d5 ♕xf7 21.♖xf7 ♗xd5 22.♖f2 ♖e1+ 23.♖f1 ♖e2 White must either agree to a draw by repetition or go for a double-edged position after 24.♗f2 ♖xb2. However, Fedoseev had looked a little further.

20.♕f5+! ♕xf5

No choice, since 20...♔b8 won't work in view of 21.d5. Or 20...♔d8? 21.♘h4+ ♔e8 22.♕c8, mate.

21.♖xf5 ♖xg2+ 22.♔f1 ♖xb2 23.♖f2

The active rook is pushed away from the second rank, and in this position, two pawns are not sufficient compensation for the knight. Despite stubborn resistance, Black had to admit defeat on the 62nd move.

Dubov's Game of the Year

The fate of the gold medal was decided in the final round, in which both leaders were black. If they finished with an equal number of points, they would have to play a rapid tie-break – just like 10 years ago, when Karjakin and Nepomniachtchi played a memorable tiebreak that was only decided in the Armageddon game, when luck smiled on Ian... This time fate decided otherwise.

Ian Nepomniachtchi played black in his last game against Maxim Chigaev, who had lost painfully the day before, after having had a large advantage. It was clear that Maxim was upset and didn't want to go for broke, so their game ended in a draw already on the 10th move.

Now Ian turned spectator and started waiting for what would happen to Karjakin, who had black against Daniil Dubov. According to Nepomniachtchi, except for a draw, he would have been satisfied with either result. By the end of the championship, tiredness had grown into exhaustion, and he did not really want to play a tie-break. Daniil Dubov did not

disappoint and there was no draw in his game against Karjakin. Instead, Dubov played a masterpiece that many pundits dubbed 'The Game of the Year'.

NOTES BY
Daniil Dubov

Daniil Dubov
Sergey Karjakin
Moscow 2020 (11)
Giuoco Piano

1.e4 e5 2.♘f3 ♘c6 3.♗c4 ♗c5 4.c3 ♘f6 5.d4 exd4 6.b4!?

Sasha Riazantsev and I looked at this for quite some time after I had mentioned it as an amusing line for a blitz game. Sasha has a very specific sense of humour and, after laughing for 10 minutes, he came up with some deep analysis.

All in all, the line looks decent for White; I don't see a way for Black to get an advantage, which is quite something for such a sharp position! I was pretty sure that Oleg Skvortsov (sponsor of, amongst others, the Zurich Chess Challenge and the Nutcracker matches of the generations in Moscow – ed.) had discovered this line, but it turns out that people were already trying it centuries before him! Still, big credit to Oleg, who actually has a lot of interesting opening ideas.

6...♗b6 6...♗e7!?, followed by 7.e5 ♘e4, is also a normal reaction.

7.e5

7...♘e4!? We thought Karjakin would be quite likely to play this, and the move is absolutely fine, but 7...d5! still seems more ambitious.

There are hundreds of crazy lines there, which I'll ignore, but I must mention the stem game of the line: 8.exf6 dxc4 9.♕e2+ ♗e6 10.b5 ♘b4 11.fxg7 ♖g8 12.cxb4 ♕f6 13.0-0 ♕xg7 14.g3 0-0-0 15.a4 d3 16.♕b2

ANALYSIS DIAGRAM

16...♕xg3+ 17.hxg3 ♖xg3+ 18.♔h2 ♖xf3 19.♗g5 ♗d4 20.♕d2 ♖g8 21.♖a3 h6 22.♖g1 ♖h3+ 23.♔g2 ♖xg5+ 24.♔f1 ♖xg1+ 25.♔xg1 ♗d5 26.♖a1 0-1, Skvortsov-Anand, Zurich 2017. Inspiring chess by both players!

8.♗d5! The key idea. Black is slightly better, with zero risk, after 8.0-0?! d5 9.exd6 0-0.

On the final day, Daniil Dubov also defeated the other front-runner, Sergey Karjakin. Again Dubov and Alexander Riazantsev came up with an original idea in the opening.

8...♘xc3 9.♘xc3 dxc3 10.♗g5 ♘e7 11.0-0 The first critical position.

11...h6! It's very important to include this, because after 11...0-0 12.♗b3 h6 White doesn't need to retreat now: 13.♕d3!.
12.♗h4

12...0-0 A very logical move and hard to criticize, but 12...g5!? was probably better, even though it still looks like a strange mess after 13.♘xg5! hxg5 14.♗xg5 d6 15.♕f3 ♗e6 16.♗xb7 d5 17.♗c6+ ♘xc6 18.♗xd8 ♔xd8 19.♕xc3, and White doesn't seem to be worse.
13...♘xd5!? is also decent. We could spend weeks looking at the complications here, so I'll show one of the lines I liked at home, just to make you understand what an unbelievable amount of work Sasha had done: 14.♘f3 ♘e7 15.♗f6 ♖g8 16.♖e1 a5 17.♕c2 axb4 18.♕h7 b3 19.♖ad1! ♗xf2+! 20.♔f1! ♗xe1 21.e6 ♖f8 22.♘e5 dxe6 23.♖xd8+ ♔xd8 24.♘xf7+

ANALYSIS DIAGRAM

24...♔e8! 25.♘d6+ ♔d7 26.♕xe7+ ♔c6 27.♕xf8 b2 28.♘e4 b1♕ 29.♕c5+ ♔d7 30.♕e7+, with a perpetual.
13.♖e1

13...♕e8?!
Again very logical, since Black wants to unpin himself, but he should probably have started with ...a5: 13...a5! 14.♕d3 axb4 15.♗b3 ♕e8 16.♗f6 ♖a3!. This is why Black needed to go ...a5 – it turns out that the rook can eliminate the bishop now: 17.♘h4 ♖xb3 18.axb3 ♔h8 19.♕h3 (the threat is ♘g6+!) 19...♔h7 20.♕d3+, and it's an amusing perpetual.
14.♗b3 a5?!
14...♘f5! was Black's last chance to keep equality, although here it's way more challenging for Black: 15.♕d3 d5 16.exd6 ♕d7 17.♖ad1

ANALYSIS DIAGRAM

17...cxd6! (17...♕xd6? runs into the beautiful 18.♕b1! ♘xh4 19.♖xd6 ♘xf3+ 20.gxf3 cxd6 21.♕d3, and Black is probably lost) 18.♗c2 ♕c6 19.♗f6!, and the attack continues.
15.♗f6!
Here we see the difference. 15.♕d3

would transpose to 13...a5, but White doesn't need to go 15.♕d3 !

15...a4 Now 15...♘f5!? leads to a crushing attack after 16.g4! gxf6 17.gxf5 d5 18.♔h1!, and White should win with accurate play. Here's one of the lines: 18...♔h7 19.♗c2 ♕e7 20.e6 ♗xf2 21.♖e2 ♗b6 22.♘e5! ♖g8 23.exf7 ♖g1+ 24.♕xg1 ♗xg1 25.♖xg1 ♕f8 26.♖eg2 ♗d7 27.♖g6, and wins.

16.♗c4 ♘g6
The knight goes to g6, since ...♘f5 will always run into g4. And now we get to the second critical point.

17.♕d3?
Very logical, especially knowing that the queen belongs on d3 in most lines, but it's a big mistake nevertheless. There were two ways to win.
Personally, I think the simplest was 17.♕c2! d5 18.exd6 ♗e6 19.♗xc3 cxd6 20.♕xg6!, and White gets a much better version of the endgame than in the game: 20...fxg6 21.♖xe6 ♕f7 22.♖xg6 ♕xc4 23.♖xg7+ ♔h8 24.♖c7+ ♕xc3 25.♖xc3, and White should win easily, since Black has too many weak pawns besides being a pawn down.
17.♘h4!? would probably win as well:

Our man on the spot Vladimir Barsky interviews Russian champion Ian Nepomniachtch His short last-round draw proved an effective gamble as he indeed avoided a tiebreak

17...♘xh4 18.♕g4 ♘f5 19.♗d3 g6 20.♗xf5 d5 21.exd6 ♗xf5 22.♕f4!

and Black has to give up his queen: 22...♔h7 23.♖xe8 ♖fxe8 24.♕c4 ♗e6 25.♕xc3 cxd6 26.♕f3, and the engine is quite sure that White should win, although it's less obvious to me than after 17.♕c2.

17...d5! 18.exd6 ♗e6
One more critical point. (Sorry if I am being too dogmatic.)

19.♕xg6! A cool move to play, but I'm actually left with nothing else.
Now there is no 19.♗xc3, since 19...♗xc4! is a tempo, unlike in the 17.♕c2 line.
And 19.♗xe6 ♘f4!, followed by ...fxe6!, is just fine for Black – this is what I had originally missed.

19...fxg6 20.♖xe6

20...♕f7? The last mistake of the game. Despite not being as smart as most commentators, I understand his decision very well. Normally, in any random position, you'd prefer an extra queen to a tough pawn-down endgame, especially when victory wins you the tournament. Maybe I'm just being stupid, though.
20...♕c6! was a must, when Black has real chances to survive after 21.♖e7+ ♕xc4 22.♖xg7+ ♔h8 23.♖xc7+ ♖xf6 24.♖xc4 ♖xd6 25.♖xc3 (here his

pawn structure is much better than after 17.♕c2) 25...♗d4 26.♘xd4 ♖xd4 27.a3 ♖ad8 28.♔f1. White is better, of course, but the game is far from won.

21.♗xc3! ♔h8 22.♖e4! ♕f5 23.♖e7 After this powerful move sequence Black is lost.

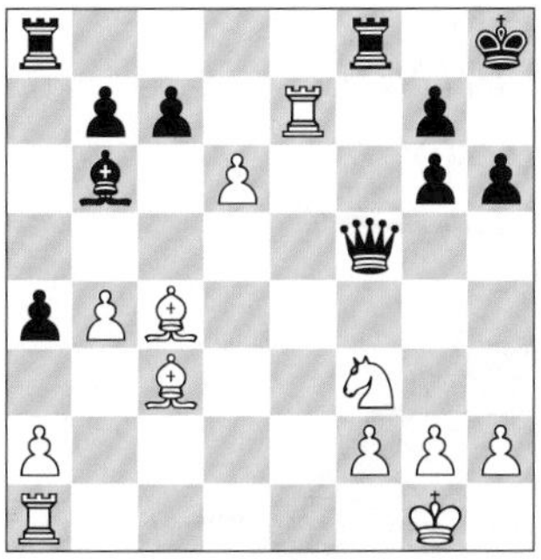

23...♖g8

23...♗xf2+!? was an amusing attempt, but it's still lost after 24.♔h1 ♖fe8!! 25.♖f7! cxd6 26.♗xg7+ ♔h7 27.♖xf5 gxf5 28.♗b2.

I was a bit worried about 23...♖f6, but 24.d7! just wins: 24...♔h7 25.♗d3.

24.♗xg8 ♖xg8 25.dxc7 ♕c2

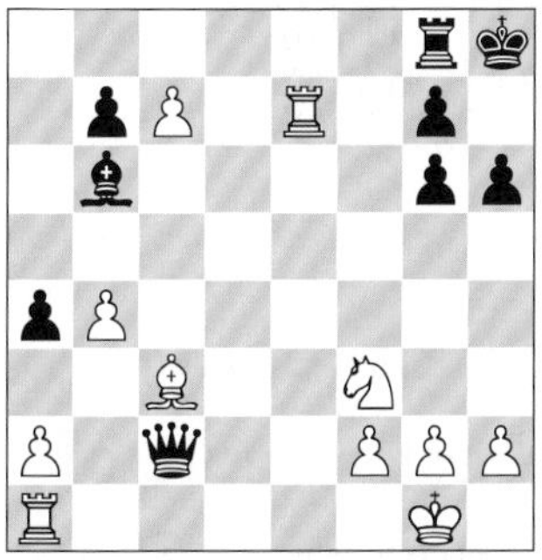

26.♗e5!

He had probably missed this idea. Now Black has almost no moves, since the rook has to defend g7, so White will slowly but surely win.

26...♗xf2+ 27.♔h1 ♗b6 28.h3

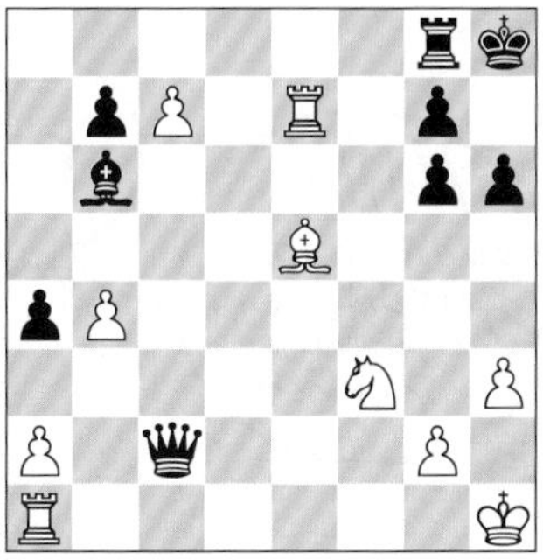

A bit of luft first...

28...♔h7 29.♖e1 a3 30.♔h2 g5 31.♘d4 And now we bring in all the pieces.

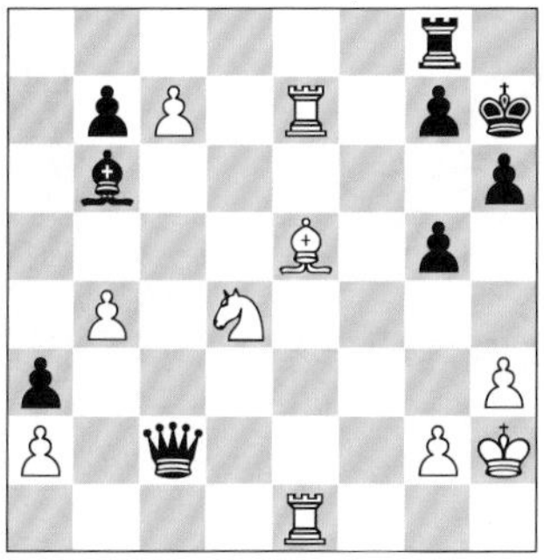

31...♕c4 32.♘f5 ♕xb4 33.♖c1 ♔g6 34.♖xg7+!

Not exactly a bright finish, but it brings home the point.

It's never too late to allow a good defender to survive. After 34.♘d6?? ♗d4! 35.♗g3 ♗f2! Black all of a sudden saves himself.

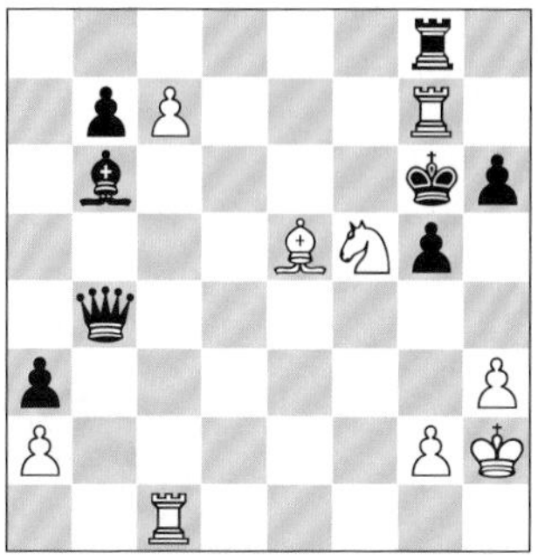

34...♔xf5 Or 34...♖xg7 35.c8♕, and wins. **35.♖xg8 ♗xc7 36.♗xc7 ♕b2 37.♖c5+ ♔e4 38.♖d8!?**

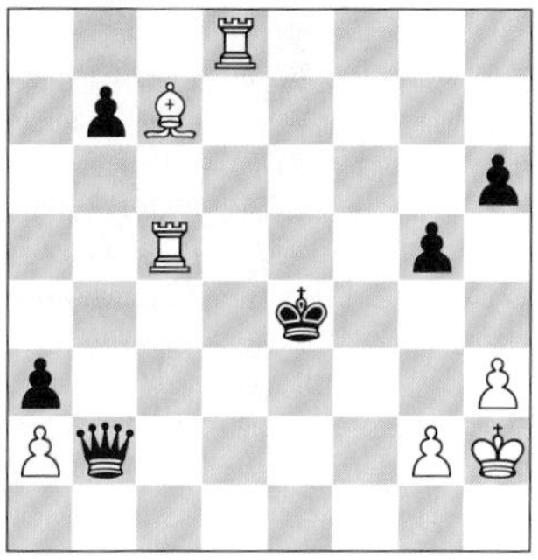

And with 39.♖e5+ coming, Sergey resigned.

■ ■ ■

Dubov's conclusion

Thanks to Daniil Dubov's brilliant creative achievement, Ian Nepomniachtchi became Russian Champion for the second time. This is how Dubov summed up what had happened: 'I would like to say that Karjakin is a great fellow. In the fight for first place, he showed a great desire to play. He played many difficult games and fought with everyone. It is true that I sometimes criticized him for some other things, but here he made a huge impression in a sporting way. As it turned out, someone went for an absolutely unforced draw after six moves and took clear first place, while someone else fought and lost. It happens.' ■

Moscow 2020 **cat. XVIII**

					1	2	3	4	5	6	7	8	9	10	11	12		TPR
1	Ian Nepomniachtchi	IGM	RUS	2784	*	1	½	0	½	½	½	½	1	1	1	1	7½	2813
2	Sergey Karjakin	IGM	RUS	2752	0	*	½	0	½	1	1	1	½	1	½	1	7	2785
3	Vladimir Fedoseev	IGM	RUS	2674	½	½	*	1	½	½	½	½	½	1	½	½	6½	2755
4	Daniil Dubov	IGM	RUS	2702	1	1	0	*	0	½	½	½	1	½	1	½	6½	2753
5	Maksim Chigaev	IGM	RUS	2619	½	½	½	1	*	1	½	½	½	0	0	1	6	2731
6	Vladislav Artemiev	IGM	RUS	2711	½	0	½	½	0	*	½	½	1	1	½	1	6	2723
7	Nikita Vitiugov	IGM	RUS	2720	½	0	½	½	½	½	*	½	½	½	1	½	5½	2686
8	Peter Svidler	IGM	RUS	2723	½	0	½	½	½	½	½	*	½	½	½	1	5½	2686
9	Andrey Esipenko	IGM	RUS	2686	0	½	½	0	½	0	½	½	*	½	1	1	5	2653
10	Maxim Matlakov	IGM	RUS	2698	0	0	0	½	1	0	½	½	½	*	1	1	5	2652
11	Aleksey Goganov	IGM	RUS	2594	0	½	½	0	1	½	0	½	0	0	*	½	3½	2565
12	Mikhail Antipov	IGM	RUS	2611	0	0	½	½	0	0	½	0	0	0	½	*	2	2434

Note: Mikhail Antipov tested positive for Covid-19 after 6 rounds and had to withdraw

New In Chess Swindle Award
And the winner is...

Swindles are the new brilliancies, or so we thought as readers enthusiastically replied to our call to send in their best swindle of 2020. Expert par excellence **DAVID SMERDON**, author of *The Complete Chess Swindler*, selected the most baffling entry.

Throughout the horrors of 2020, bookended by the Australian bushfires and the UK cancelling Christmas, I have been gratefully uplifted by a steady stream of amateur chess swindles from around the world. This began after my article in New In Chess 2020/1, when readers were invited to send in their favourite swindles from their own games.

Some of these gems snuck into the final manuscript of *The Complete Chess Swindler* before it hit the printers; others were featured in New In Chess 2020/5. This follow-up article ended with the editors generously announcing a 'New In Chess Swindle Award' to discover the swindle of the year, which resulted in more virtual nourishment over the second half of 2020.

Since I started collecting swindles five years ago, I've noticed that this topic is universally enjoyed by chess players. The stories that filled my inbox were written with as much enthusiasm and drama as a sporting miracle or a Hollywood thriller, complete with villains and heroes, highs and lows, plot twists and resolutions. One annotated game by a high-profile Jamaican attorney read like a scene from a Tolkien novel. The renowned endgame expert GM Karsten Müller sent me an historic swindle from 1997, without which he opines that he may never have earned his final GM norm and subsequently written his decorated *Fundamental Chess Endings*. Everyone seems to have a swindle story, from the unluckiest amateur to the most decorated champion (though, disappointingly, Magnus didn't send in anything).

Judging any 'Best...' necessarily entails a degree of subjectivity, and swindles are no exception. New In Chess placed no restrictions on what sort of games could be submitted, which was fortunate, given that practically all chess last year ended up being played online. I considered all submitted games from 2020 for the award, though I placed slightly more weight on longer time-controls and more serious tournaments. But my main criteria revolved around the swindle itself, including:

■ Actively encouraging a blunder by way of the swindle setup.
■ Use of chess psychology, such as creating fear or chaos over the board or deliberately playing moves that meet with engine disapproval.
■ Creativity and depth of the swindle.
■ Magnitude of the lost position.

And the winner of the €250 New In Chess Swindle Award is... Kyron Griffith! The winning entry was played in a chess.com league match in November 2020, between the Mechanics' Institute Chess Club, based in California, and the University of Texas Rio Grande Valley Rising Stars. While it was played at a rapid control of 15 min + 2 sec, the game is memorable for the way that Black conjures up chances out of the abyss. Lost by move 12, he never gives up and continues to set problems for his opponent, even when finding himself a full queen down for 10 straight moves. Courage, creativity and psychology combine to produce enough pressure that White falls for the final, outrageously brazen tactic.

Lost by move 12, he never gives up, even when finding himself a full queen down for 10 straight moves

'indirect'
Kyron Griffith
chess.com MICC v RGVRS 2020
Caro-Kann, Advance Variation

1.e4 c6 2.d4 d5 3.e5 ♗f5 4.♘c3 e6 5.g4 ♗g6 6.♘ge2 c5 7.h4 h5 8.♘f4 ♗h7 9.♘xh5 cxd4
The little that I know about this variation is that 9...♘c6! is supposed to give Black quite good compensation for the pawn.
10.♘b5! ♗c5?! 10...♘c6! 11.♘xd4 ♘ge7, with compensation.
11.♘xd4 ♘c6?
It's 'third try unlucky' for this move. Black intended to meet 12.♘xg7+ with ...♔f8??, but realized too late that this allows a killer fork on e6.
12.♘xg7+ ♔d7 13.♘xc6 bxc6 14.♘h5

White is a healthy two pawns to the good. The position is still a bit messy and one could argue that White's king is at least as exposed as its counterpart on d7, but it's White's point to lose from here. If Black is to have any chances of a swindle, he needs to immediately go on the initiative before White has time to finish his development.
14...♗e4 15.♖h3 ♕b6 16.♕e2 a5!

Prophylactic swindling (Dvoretsky would be proud). Now if 17.♖b3 Black can play 17...♕a7 followed by ...a4, while this possibility also gives White a reason to think twice about a potential queenside fianchetto.
17.c3 ♖b8!
Keeping the pressure on to tie down White's dark-squared bishop. Black continues to try to make his opponent's conversion as difficult (or at the very least annoying) as possible.
18.b3 ♔c7
Up until now, the clock times have been pretty similar – both sides have about ten minutes left plus the two-second increment. But across the next few moves, White starts to have some reasonably big thinks as he struggles to untangle his pieces while navigating his opponent's threats.
**19.♘g3 ♗h7 20.♘h5 ♖d8?
21.♗g5! ♖b8 22.♗g2**
So, Black has given White two tempi to complete his development. But the game goes on...
22...♘e7 23.♖d1 ♘c8

+6, says Stockfish.
24.f4?! There's nothing particular wrong with this move, but it does mean that the white king is unlikely

Resignation would be the default reply here. But don't stop reading!

to ever find complete safety in the middlegame. I would have opted for the conservative 24.♔f1 and maybe even continued a regal march to the corner.

24...♗e7 25.♘f6 ♗xf6 26.exf6?! Again, this move is not objectively weak – the evaluation is still pushing towards +6. But why allow Black's dismal knight a glimpse of greener pastures?

26...♘d6! 27.c4 27.f5! ♖be8 28.♖e3 exf5 29.♖e7+ ♔c8 30.♕e5 was a particularly clinical winning line.

27...♗e4! 28.♔f1 a4! 29.f5! exf5? 30.♗e3 ♕a6? 31.♗f4! The temporary pawn sacrifice leads to a decisive attack on the dark

squares. Black is completely lost, but his next move is still a howler:

31...axb3?? Allowing a simple two-mover. **32.♗xd6+ ♔xd6 33.c5+** Winning the queen. Resignation would be the default reply here. But don't stop reading!

33...♔e5 Why not? At least Black can claim the moral victory in the 'King of the Hill' variant.

34.♕xa6 b2! 35.♗xe4 dxe4 36.♖b3 Here 36.♕xc6 was the fastest route to checkmate, but

why calculate when you can trade? **36...fxg4!?** Creating a third passed pawn. You may find this an absurd comment, but this little pawn will one day steal the show.

37.♕xc6 ♖xb3 38.axb3

Not the sort of diagram you see every day in this magazine...

38...♖xh4 39.♕d6+ (If you want a quick calculation exercise, there's a mate in 8 beginning with 39.♖d5+, all checks.)

39...♔f5 40.♖d5+? ♔g6 41.♖d1

41...♔f5!
White had invited Black to 'win' material with 41...♖h1+. But White's task becomes childishly simple after 42.♔e2 b1♕ 43.♖xb1 ♖xb1 44.c6.
42.♔g2 Many of us would have surely played 42.c6. But let's not ruin the performance.
42...♖h3!! Exclamation marks for a move that allows mate in 6.
43.c6

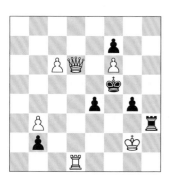

43...♖d3!! 44.♖xd3?
White used half of his remaining minute on this decision, presumably most of which was shock recovery. Under the pressure of the game situation, White misses that the alternative capture was a trivial solution. 44.♕xd3! exd3 45.c7.
From the comfort of our chairs, we may feel emboldened to write off the final result as the sole product of White's mistakes, such as this one. Let's not be so naive. White missed several wins, to be sure, but these omissions were the direct result of the pressure created by Black, whose tenacity, optimism and imagination have already kept the game going a good 30 moves since it was first 'resign-able'. Swindling is not about luck!

44...b1♕
Black has somehow managed to make a new queen and is now 'only' a rook down (with mate in 11 at White's disposal as well).
45.♖d2 ♔g6!
With an ironic hat tip to the classical masters, Griffith explains: 'Prophylaxis – not giving White any checks, for maximum swindling chances.'
46.c7 ♕xb3 47.♖f2
Avoiding even the faintest whiff of a perpetual check as the tenths-of-seconds ticked down. But after 47.c8♕ ♕f3+ 48.♔g1 ♕e3+ 49.♖f2 ♕e1+ 50.♔g2 there are no more checks.
47...♕h3+ 48.♔g1 e3! 49.c8♕ exf2+ 50.♔xf2

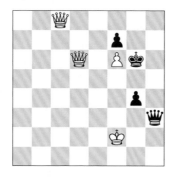

50...g3+!!
An illusion of diabolical proportions. As we all know, backward-diagonal moves are the hardest to see in chess. Having suffered through multiple stunning surprises, and with only 17 seconds on his clock, White finally blunders away the win.
51.♔e1??
51.♕xg3+, of course, but I have run out of witty comments.
51...♕xc8 52.♕xg3+ ♔xf6
The endgame is drawn, quite easily in fact. But given the two-second increment and what had just transpired, 'somehow it felt like both players knew that Black would win now', writes Griffith.
53.♕f4+ ♕f5 54.♕h4+ ♔e5 55.♕h8+ ♔e4 56.♕b8 ♕e5 57.♕b3 ♔f4+ 58.♔f1 f6 59.♕d3 ♕a1+ 60.♔g2 ♕b2+ 61.♔f1 ♕c1+ 62.♔g2 ♕c6+

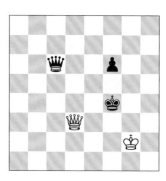

63.♔f1??
It was inevitable.
63...♕f3+ 64.♕xf3+ ♔xf3 65.♔e1 ♔g2 66.♔e2 f5 67.♔e3 ♔g3 68.♔e2 f4 69.♔e1 ♔g2 70.♔e2 f3+ 71.♔e1 f2+ 0-1.
A terrific rollercoaster of a game. Make no mistake that this was just a 'lucky' win. Black never stopped fighting and created his own luck. A true Swindler deserves every point.

Honourable Mention
The number of entries was heart-warming and the level high. Many deserve to appear in print and hopefully they will in a next edition of my book. Here's an honourable mention that I might have dubbed 'best Tal-like Swindle'. Played at a mature 45 min + 15 sec / move, the inaugural German Online Chess League was a joint initiative of the German Chess Federation and ChessBase and the competition will be renewed for 2021. The top-board clash from the third division match between SC Fulda and SV Dresden-Striesen saw a game that is less chaotic than the winner, but still features a healthy (and subtle) dose of psychological lead-up play that culminates in a fabulous finale.

Martin Weise
Bernhard Scheuermann
chessbase.com 2020
Caro-Kann, Panov Attack

1.♘f3 c5 2.e3 ♘c6 3.d4 cxd4 4.exd4 d5 5.c4 ♘f6 6.♘c3 e6 7.cxd5 exd5 8.♗g5
However stale the position looks, Black has to be careful. With the kings still on the e-file, the extra

"Jan Timman's games reflect his adventurous outlook on life. He plays in a swashbuckling style, but always underpinned with a great strategic and positional sense. You will find great positional wins and fantastic attacking chess. Timman is absolutely fearless, always prepared to sacrifice material for the initiative and for the attack. But he also enjoys the beauty in chess. The games are mainly described in words, with variations given only when things get critical. Magnificent."
GM Daniel King, Power Play Chess

"A fascinating journey through more than 50 years from the good old days to modern computer times. But his play is the same: always fighting and creative. A worthy successor to Timman's Titans."
GM Karsten Müller, author of Bobby Fischer: The Career and Complete Games

"Lots of splendid games. The annotations are pleasantly easygoing with short variations in which Timman balances the computer evaluation with profound comments on the practical and human aspects of the position's essence. The large number of games with black is striking: Timman always played for a win, with both colours."
IM Jeroen Bosch, Schaakmagazine

"Timman's annotations are up to his usual high standard. There is plenty of prose, including anecdotes of his friends and colleagues, and not many longer lines of analysis. This book is definitely a triumph for Jan Timman."
Sean Marsh, CHESS Magazine

"A new and splendid book by Jan Timman. Once again he shows his ability to

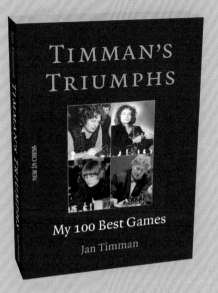

reveal in deep analysis the hidden truth in the games. Of course, in between the games there is ample room for fascinating history and anecdotes."
Bab Wilders, Nederlands Dagblad

"Recounts the career of the best player in the West for much of the 1970s and 80s. This is a book that belongs in the library of every chess player."
IM John Donaldson

"Timman has always been a universal player who uses a wide range of openings so there's a lot of variety in the play: no chance of getting bored by seeing the same type of position over and over again. Each game is put into its context regarding the tournament or match in which it took place. The text is also enlivened by many entertaining anecdotes, often concerning Timman's rather hedonistic (especially in his early years) lifestyle. We read, for instance, about listening to Frank Zappa with Ray Keene, and taking the young Nigel Short to a nightclub on the eve of an important game. There are many readers who particularly enjoy best games collections: they will certainly revel in this excellent book. For those of you of Timman's (and my) generation the book will also bring back many

memories. For younger readers, though, much of it will be ancient history: perhaps they'll get the same pleasure out of it that I got from studying the games of Alekhine and Capablanca many years ago."
Richard James, British Chess News

"Besides a collection of 100 beautifully annotated games, this book is also an ode to freedom, the freedom of the days when Timman became a professional chess player."
GM Hans Ree, NRC Handelsblad

"Timman is one of the most diligent and most accomplished authors of his gild. Self-criticism comes natural to him. Timman presents his games chronologically and takes the reader on a journey through his career of more than 50 years. Particularly fascinating are those passages in which he characterizes his competitors. His style of analysis is very pleasant. If you buy a Timman book it is very unlikely you will be disappointed."
Harry Schaack, KARL Magazine

"Here they are: the best hundred games of 'Best of the West' Jan Timman. And they surpass all expectations. How pure and logic was the style he managed to express in his best games, and how do some of his games resemble a flawless strategic accomplishment. I was aware that that Timman's endgames were of exceptional quality, but he is also able to ruthlessly knock out famous players if they make a small, almost undetectable error. Timman's chess is elegant, extremely well-considered and beautiful and this collection is full of gems. The book is, I dare say, a triumph."
Florian Jacobs, Max Euwe Center

352 pages | paperback €32.95 | also available as NIC Interactive eBook | a **NEW IN CHESS** publication

tempo can sometimes provide White the chance to turn the symmetry into a pleasant positional advantage.

8...♗e7 9.♗b5 0-0 10.0-0 ♗e6?
10...♗g4!. **11.♗xc6! bxc6 12.♘e5**
♕c7? A bad positional mistake. Black's position was a little uncomfortable, but with 12...♖c8! he still could have maintained good chances of equalising. Now the c-pawn becomes a permanent weakness.
13.♖c1 ♗d6??

The only thing worse than a positional mistake is a tactical one.
14.♘b5! ♕b8 15.♘xd6 ♕xd6
16.♗xf6 gxf6 17.♖xc6

A straightforward combination sees White up a pawn, with a better

The only thing worse than a positional mistake is a tactical one

structure and superior minor piece to boot. Scheuermann writes about his thoughts at this moment: 'Should I resign? Yes, that's an option, but let's postpone that decision for some moves.' In fact, Black does far more than just go through the motions over his next few moves. The first task when entering 'swindle mode' is to take stock of your strengths and weaknesses. Starting with the latter, Black identifies that he has lost the battle for the queen-side and that he should try to avoid trades. On the other hand, he does possess the potential of a semi-open file aimed at the white king. With few prospects of a normal defence, Black switches all attention to the kingside:
17...♕b8! 18.♘g4 ♕f4! 19.♘e3
A very secure square for the knight, wouldn't you agree?

19...♖ab8!!
I like this move a lot because, from a psychological perspective, it encourages the reply that will prove to be the cause of White's later regrets. White has several ways to deal with the threat to the pawn on b2, but each has its perceived drawbacks:
– 20.♕c2 (or ♕e2) drops the pawn on d4.
– 20.b3 allows the potentially annoying ...♖b4.
– 20.♖c2 retreats White's most active piece.

– 20.g3 (followed by 21.♕d2) weakens the light squares.
Intuitively, White's next move, which 'only' self-pins the knight on e3, is the logical choice. This, we shall see, is a key component of the swindle to come.
20.♕d2 ♔h8! Continuing the migration to the kingside.
21.♖fc1 ♖g8!
And here comes the swindle!

22.b3?? White frees up his queen from the defence of b2, banking on his kingside being well enough defended to ignore for at least one more move. For example, 22...♗h3 23.g3! and everything's covered. But one move is all Black needs to turn this game on its head.
22...♖xg2+!! Shattering the illusion of White's defences. **23.♔xg2** 23.♘xg2? ♕xd2. **23...♗h3+!! 24.♔xh3 ♖g8!**

The white king has been fatally drawn out into No Man's Land, from which there is no way back. White resigned. Possibly White missed that he could keep the game going with a double rook sacrifice: 25.♖xf6 ♕xf6 26.♖c6!. But there follows a nice echo of the final position: 26...♕f3+! 27.♔h4 ♕f4+ 28.♔h3 f6! and mate on h6. ∎

Memorable meetings
with the Magician

In 1976, Mikhail Tal approached a rising star from Lviv and invited him to play a training match, attracted as he was by the young man's 'tasty chess'. Now, for the first time, **OLEG ROMANISHIN** writes about this and a second training match with 'the Magician from Riga', reliving a dear memory from which he emerged with a positive score.

As a young boy, I grew up surrounded by a love for chess. My father was an electrical engineer by profession, with a passion for the game. He was a first-category player and had participated in the Lviv championships in the 1930s and '40s.

His best result, I believe, was third place. He stopped playing competitive chess when his children were born, but he taught all of us the rules. My older siblings quickly lost interest, but I, the youngest, liked the game.

I learned to play at the age of five, and my father started playing handicap matches against me. He began by giving me queen and two rooks, and when I quickly scored my first win, the next handicap was queen, rook and minor piece. And so he continued. Next was queen and rook, then queen and minor piece. Whenever I started winning, he would reduce the odds.

By the time we played our first normal game, I was seven years old. We recorded the score. I lost the first 99 games with equal material, and then, in the 100th game, I made a draw! I think he did this on purpose. He wanted to teach me to lose. He wanted me to be ready to lose a game. Of course, this approach also contained a risk. You must overcome your losses, but you mustn't get used to losing – or tire of the game. Still, despite those 99 losses I didn't lose interest and continued to be ready to fight. Most children would have lost interest, and that would be it, but I still wanted to win. Some 40 years ago, when I was a grandmaster, a Polish journalist asked me what had been my first success. I said, when I scored this first draw against my father. And that was true.

Glued to the radio
We had a lot of chess books at home, and I devoured them. Everybody in our family knew how to play, and we all followed the important tourna-

> **Oleg Romanishin crossed swords with eight World Champions. The largest number of official games (23) he played against Mikhail Tal.**

ments on the radio and in the newspapers. My father made cross-tables of the Interzonals and the Candidates tournaments. We looked at the games of the World Championship matches between Botvinnik and Smyslov in 1957, and Botvinnik and Tal in 1961, as they were published in the newspapers. Starting with the title match between Botvinnik and Petrosian in 1963, it was possible to follow the games on the radio. We wrote down the moves as we listened, analysed the positions and tried to guess the next moves. I didn't have a favourite player at the time, but already in 1959, during the Candidates tournament in Yugoslavia, while the other members of my family were rooting for Keres,

I was rooting for Tal. I wanted Tal to win – which he did, ahead of Keres – but I don't recall why.

Autographs
In 1962, the annual traditional friendly match between the USSR and Yugoslavia was held in Lviv. Every day I went there to collect autographs from Gligoric, Ivkov, Matanovic, Taimanov and Stein, who was from Lviv. Of course, I didn't dare to speak to them, because I was too shy, and

While the other members of my family were rooting for Keres, I wanted Tal to win

unfortunately I no longer have those autographs. But already then, at the age of 10, I knew the names of all the famous chess players. And like every child I had dreams. I dreamed that one day I would participate in such tournaments and cross swords with these great players.

Later, these childhood dreams started coming true. In 1971, I was lucky to play in a tournament (a round-robin!) in Gothenburg with Spassky, Hort, Szabo and Pomar. In the space of just a couple of years, such tournaments became normal, and I was fortunate to play many games against almost all the great grandmasters of the previous generation: Petrosian, Smyslov, Bronstein, Kortchnoi, Geller, Gligoric, Larsen, Portisch, and many more. Unfortunately, I 'missed' Keres by one year. His last USSR championship was in 1973, while I made my debut in 1974.

All in all, I played eight World Champions from different generations. From Smyslov to Kramnik and Anand (I am only considering the winners of title matches), a total of 73 games with a total score of +16 -20 =37. But the largest number of games, 23 in official competitions, I played against Mikhail Tal.

Getting to know Tal
The first time I saw Tal in the flesh was in Riga in 1968, during the Soviet Cup, when I played on one of

Lviv legend Leonid Stein instructs budding talents. Opposite Stein sits a very young Alexander Beliavsky, next to him (seen on the back) Oleg Romanishin.

Tal and Romanishin at the start of their first-round game in the 1975 Soviet Championship in Yerevan.

against Vaganian, he was already in trouble against Beliavsky and lost. They ended up sharing first and second place, while I won my last three games to share 5th place.

Tal and I got to know each other better in 1975, when we were both sent to a festival of the Communist newspaper of Germany [West-Germany at the time – ed.], *Unsere Zeit* (Our Time), in Düsseldorf. This was how it went in those years. We were obliged to go there, give a simul and talk to the people, and we did not receive any payment for this, except expenses and some pocket money.

Our reception at the airport of Frankfurt was slightly comical. They met us, embraced us and then asked

In the hotel Tal asked for the telephone book, found a chess club and just called them

us who we were. I told them that we were chess players and that Tal was a former World Champion. They said

the junior boards for my club Avant-garde, while he played for Daugava, his club from Riga. Six years later, in 1974, I played my first game against him in my first Soviet Championship in Leningrad. Tal won that championship together with Beliavsky. With two rounds to go, Tal was one point ahead of Beliavsky, who he would play against as White in the penultimate round. But he was afraid of

Vaganian, who was playing against me with Black and who was the runner-up at that point. Tal was afraid I could lose to Vaganian and paid more attention to our game than to his own, and didn't know what to go for. Everybody knows that this is a big mistake. You have to play your own game and not take other games into account – which is easier said than done, of course. By the time he realized that I was winning

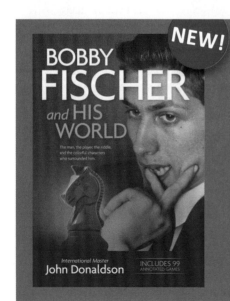

OK, and a few minutes later they started calling him Spassky! Because Spassky was the chess player they mostly read about.

When they took us to our hotel, Tal shocked them by telling them that he wanted to buy a lot of things for his little daughter, who was one year old. This was another funny episode. Tal never talked about the price, but just entered a shop and pointed at what he wanted to buy: this, this and this. He didn't care about the price; he just wanted to buy it. And the Germans couldn't understand this.

Then, in the evening, Tal wanted to go to a chess club. He always wanted to do something with chess, wherever he was. The organizers were not very eager and said it was complicated and impossible. So in the hotel Tal asked for the telephone book, found a chess club and just called them. Of course they were happy to have Tal, and they organized a blitz tournament for us that evening. I don't remember, but I suppose Tal won. He was a fantastic blitz player.

First training match
We are slowly getting close to what I wanted to write about: the two 'secret' training matches that I played

As Genna Sosonko confided to me many years later, Tal had told him that 'Romanishin plays tasty chess'

against Tal – matches that you won't find in the databases. Tal invited me to play the first training match at the end of the 1975 Soviet Championship in Yerevan, after the closing dinner. In that championship, we had played an interesting game in the first round

that ended in a draw. Tal told me later that he had been impressed by my decision in the following position:

Romanishin-Tal
Yerevan ch-USSR 1975
position after 20...♘xb7

Here I played **21.♕g4!?** offering a queen swap (which was accepted), despite the fact that I was an exchange down.

In that same championship, I had also introduced two home-prepared strong novelties; moves that won me two games and that have stood the test of time till this day: a pawn sacrifice in the Ruy Lopez against Geller and the following manoeuvre against Petrosian:

Romanishin-Petrosian
Yerevan Soviet Championship 1975
position after 5.♗d3!?

Petrosian won the championship, and this was the only game he lost. Tal and I were amongst four players who shared second place half a point adrift. Attracted by my play, Tal invited me to a training camp that he planned to have in Jurmala in the

summer of 1976, where he wanted to prepare for the upcoming Interzonal in Biel. As Genna Sosonko confided to me many years later, Tal had told him that 'Romanishin plays tasty chess'. Maybe that was why he found it difficult to play against me. This is quite common when you appreciate someone's play.

Jurmala is a seaside resort on the Baltic Sea, and we were staying close to the beach at a resort of the Ministry of Health. We had all our meals at the hotel, but it was a kind of sanatorium and very dull, so we didn't want to be lodged there and stayed in a different building. We could eat there because the president of the Latvian chess federation was the Minister of Health of Latvia. He had arranged this for Tal. As usual, Tal had his family with him; he liked to travel with his family. He was with his wife, his third one, Gela (Angelina), and their daughter Zhanna. They had a suite where we played our match.

We talked a lot during our meals, which I found interesting, because he was a very educated person. We spoke about life, but also about openings, some positions, how to prepare... During our conversations we didn't speak much about politics. Tal was not a Communist, nor was he like Spassky, who maybe talked too much. But I learned many political jokes from Tal. Political jokes were normal in the Soviet Union in the '70s and '80s. In the '50s or '40s they could have got you into prison or before the firing squad, but in the '70s and '80s, intellectuals had stopped believing in any of these Communist ideas. Of course no one could expect that the Soviet Union would collapse so soon, but everyone understood what was going on and that it was propaganda. So we spoke like normal people and we trusted each other.

A lot of improvisation

As it turned out, our training match consisted of five games. Somehow we didn't manage to play more. The games were played in the afternoon. Before lunch we were busy with other things. In the evening, we would analyse the game together, including the adjourned positions, if there were any. The time-control was the usual one at that time, 2.5 hours for 40 moves.

Please don't criticize the level of the games, particularly in the opening, too hard. They were played in the 'pre-computer' era. There was a lot of improvisation on both sides. If there

was any preparation, it was mostly 'in the mind'.

The first two games ended in wins for me. In the first game, I won material with a tactical trick, but Tal missed chances to fight for a draw. The second game was my best effort.

**Oleg Romanishin
Mikhail Tal**
Jurmala 1976 (secret match, 2)
English Opening, Four Knights Variation

1.c4 e5 2.♘c3 ♘f6 3.♘f3 ♘c6 4.g3 ♗c5

This system hadn't been played very often; only a few games up to that time. Tal's great opening erudition and wide chess knowledge allowed him to play various rare lines, often things he had seen played by someone else somewhere... And he didn't use

A cartoon showing that Romanishin and Tal shared first place in Leningrad 1977.

these ideas in training games only... Of the current grandmasters with a similar approach, I would mention Vasyl Ivanchuk, with the main difference that Ivanchuk prefers to prepare first.

5.♗g2 0-0 6.0-0 d6 7.d3
I wasn't really sure whether I wanted to push the pawn to d4 at all.
7...h6 8.e3

8...a6 Also possible is 8...♗g4!? 9.h3 ♗h5, or 8...♖e8!?. And 8...a5 is playable too, even though it slightly weakens the queenside.
9.a3 ♗a7 10.b4

10...♗g4
10...♗e6 11.♘d2, with the idea of ♘d5, was Kortchnoi's recommendation here.
Lajos Portisch played another plan after 10...♗e6, preventing the bishop on g2 from being exchanged and opening the b-file by pushing the a-pawn: 11.♖e1 ♕d7 12.♖b1 ♖ad8 13.♕c2 ♘e7 14.a4. Maybe it isn't necessary to put the bishop on b2 if you don't intend to push d4 or if Black doesn't play ...d5. From d2, the bishop would defend the e3-pawn against a Black counter-attack.

leg Romanishin and Mikhail Tal answer questions from members of the Yurmula Chess ub. Next to Tal sit a Latvian official and former draughts World Champion Iser Kuperman.

I would prefer 10...♗f5, saving a tempo (compared to the game) and preventing ♘d2.
11.h3 Miton-David, Greek team championship 2014, saw 11.♕c2 ♕d7 12.♗b2 ♗h3.
11...♗e6
The alternative was 11...♗h5.

12.e4!?
An unexpected decision. White switches to active play on the kingside after having smothered Black's activities in the centre. The black bishop on a7 shouldn't cause White any problems.
Also possible was the traditional 12.♗b2!?, when 12...e4 13.♘xe4 ♘xe4 14.dxe4 ♗xe4 15.♖e1 would be clearly in White's favour.

12...♘d4 13.♗e3 ♕d7 Another idea was 13...c6. **14.♗xd4** Note that 14.♔h2? would be a mistake: 14...♘xf3+ 15.♕xf3 ♘g4+! 16.hxg4 ♗xg4 17.♗h3, and this saves the queen, but ends up losing a pawn after 17...♗xh3.

14...exd4 It would probably have been better to refuse the pawn offer and exchange the 'bad' bishop with 14...♗xd4 15.♘xd4 exd4 16.♘e2 ♗xh3 17.♘xd4, although White gets some space advantage, of course.
15.♘e2 ♗xh3 16.♗xh3
There was no reason to recapture the d4-pawn and activate the a7-bishop. White now gets a piece majority for an attack on the kingside and the open h-file.

16...♕xh3 17.♘f4 ♕d7 18.♔g2 b5 Trying to get counterplay, but creating additional weaknesses in the black position.
19.cxb5 axb5 20.♖h1

20...♖fe8? It was better to bring a second rook to the defence of the kingside with 20...♖ae8. The rook on a8 is doing nothing there.
21.♘h5 ♘g4? Missing a tactic. Better was 21...♖e6. Black is lost now.
22.♘h4 ♖e5 23.♘xg7

23...♖g5 Since 23...♔xg7 runs into 24.♘f5+ ♖xf5 25.♕xg4+, and White wins. **24.♘gf5 ♔f8 25.♕d2 ♕e6 26.♕f4 ♕f6 27.♘f3 ♖g6 28.a4**

Exploiting the poor position of rook a8, White also gets a passed pawn.

28...♗b6 29.a5 ♗a7 30.♖ac1 c5 31.bxc5 ♗xc5 31...dxc5 is also met by 32.♖h4. **32.♖h4 ♘e5 33.♘xe5 dxe5 34.♕d2 ♗e7 35.♖c7 ♗d8 36.♕b4+ ♔g8 37.♖d7 ♕e6 38.♖d6**

38...♕xd6 39.♘xd6 ♗xh4 40.♕c5 b4 41.♘xf7
Black resigned.

In the third game, we repeated the opening of the first game, a sub-line of the French Defence. I deviated with a daring pawn push on move 5, which led to more interesting play. That game ended in a draw, but I should have lost.

Mikhail Tal
Oleg Romanishin
Jurmala 1976 (secret match, 3)
French Defence

1.e4 e6 2.d4 d5 3.♘c3 ♗e7 4.e5 c5 5.♕g4 g5!?
An adventurous move and more interesting than 5...g6, which I had played in the first game. Some people prefer 5...♔f8 here.

6.♕h5
I have found only one other game

in which 5...g5 was played, and that game continued 6.dxc5!? h5 7.♕d1 ♘c6 8.♘f3 g4 9.♘d4 ♘xe5 10.♘db5 a6 11.♘d6+ ♗xd6 12.cxd6 ♕xd6 13.♗e3 ♘d7 14.♕d2 0-0-0 15.0-0-0 f6, and Black was a pawn up in Young-Driessens, European Clubs 2013.
6...cxd4 7.♘b5

7...a6?
Better was 7...♘c6 8.♘f3 first, and only then 8...a6 9.♘bxd4 (or 9.♕xg5!? ♘xe5 10.♘xe6 ♗xe6 11.♕xe5 ♗f6 12.♘c7+ ♔d7 13.♘xe6 fxe6, with a complicated position) 9...♘xd4 10.♘xd4, but after 10...♕c7 11.f4 ♗b4+ 12.♔d1 gxf4 13.♗xf4 White is better anyway.
8.♘xd4 ♕b6 9.♘gf3 ♘d7 10.♗d3 h6

Now Black would be OK after 11.0-0? ♘gf6!. But:
11.♗g6!
A very unpleasant surprise. Taking loses the queen, and the pawn on f7 cannot be defended.
11...♔d8 12.♗xf7 ♘xe5 13.♗xg8 ♘xf3+ 14.♘xf3 ♕b4+ 15.♗d2 ♕e4+ 16.♔d1 ♖xg8 17.♗a5+ ♔d7 18.♖e1

Tal flashed out all these moves.
18...♕a4 19.♕f7 ♔d6 20.♕xg8 ♕xa5 21.♘d4 ♕d8 22.♕f7 ♕f8
As long as White has his rook on a1, Black still has some chances.
23.♖xe6+ ♗xe6 24.♕xe6+ ♔c7 25.♔e2!

Finally. White is two pawns up, and now all he needs to do is deploy his rook.
25...♗c5 26.♕xd5 ♔b6 27.c3 ♖d8 28.♕c4 ♕d6 29.♘b3 ♖c8 30.h3 ♕e5+ 31.♔f1 ♕h2

32.♖d1?
Missing a winning continuation: 32.♘xc5! ♖xc5 33.♕b4+ ♖b5 (or 33...♔c6 34.♕e4+ ♔b6 35.♖d1 ♖e5 36.♕d4+, and wins) 34.♕d4+ ♔c7 35.♖d1, and Black is lost.

32...♕h1+ Now Black saves the game. **33.♔e2 ♖e8+ 34.♔d2 ♖d8+ 35.♘d4 ♕xg2 36.♔c2 ♗xd4 37.cxd4 ♕xf2+**

The pawns are equal again.
38.♔b3 ♕f3+ 39.♖d3 ♕d5 40.♖e3 ♕b5+ 41.♕xb5+ ♔xb5
Draw.

The fourth game was adjourned after 42 moves. Tal, playing as Black, was about to lose a pawn and had to fight for a draw. But we didn't find time to resume play. The fifth game was the last one we played and this time, Tal won.

Mikhail Tal
Oleg Romanishin
Jurmala 1976 (secret match, 5)
French Defence, Tarrasch Variation
1.e4 e6 2.d4 d5 3.♘c3 ♗e7

4.♗d3
After 4.♘f3 ♘f6 5.♗d3 Black continues with 5...c5 or 5...dxe4.
4...♘c6 5.♘f3 ♗b4 6.♗e2
White achieves nothing with 6.0-0 ♘xd3, but could try to include 6.♗b5+ c6 7.♗e2.
6...dxe4 7.♘xe4 ♘f6 8.♘xf6+

Tilburg 1979. Oleg Romanishin, who would finish second, chats with later winner Anatoly Karpov.

♗xf6 9.c3 ♘d5 10.0-0 0-0 11.♕c2 b6 12.♕e4

12...♖b8
And not immediately 12...♗b7? in view of 13.♗d3 g6 14.♗h6 ♖e8 15.c4 ♘b4 16.♕xb7 ♘xd3 17.♕e4 ♘b4 18.a3, and White is clearly better.
13.♗d3 g6 14.♗h6 ♗g7

15.♗g5!
White should keep his pieces, use his space advantage and threaten sacrifices on g6 and e6, while attacking the black king.
15...♘e7 16.♖fe1
16.♕h4? is a mistake in view of 16...f6 17.♗h6 ♗b7 18.♗d2 ♘f5.
16...h6 17.♗h4 ♗b7
17...f5?! only favours White after 18.♗xe7 ♕xe7 19.♕e3.
18.♕g4

18...♕e8
Maybe Black should have tried 18...g5!?, as the sacrifices on g5 are not that clear.
19.♕h3 c5 20.dxc5 bxc5 21.♘e5 ♘d5 22.♗g3 ♖d8 23.♖ad1

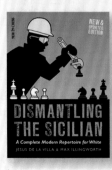

23...♘f6?! Black should have prevented White from moving his bishop to the c1-h6 diagonal. But that is easier said than done.
24.♗f4 g5 25.♗e3!? Very clever, first luring the queen to e7.
25...♕e7 26.♗c1

Now White's pieces are ready to launch an attack.
26...♖d5 27.f4 ♖fd8 28.fxg5 hxg5 29.♗xg5 c4 30.♗h7+ ♔f8 31.♖xd5 ♖xd5 32.♕e3 ♕c7 33.♗c2 ♕b6 34.♕xb6 axb6

35.♗xf6? White should not have fallen for the temptation to grab a second pawn. 35.♗c1, or even 35.h4!?, would have been good enough.
35...♗xf6 36.♘xc4

36...♖g5?
A further mistake.
After 36...b5 Black would have had chances of a draw due to his active pieces: 37.♘a5 ♖d2 38.♘xb7 ♖xc2 39.♖b1 ♗e7.
37.♗e4 ♗a6 38.♘xb6 ♗d8 39.♘a4 ♗b5 40.b3 ♖e5 41.♖d1 ♗a5 42.♖d4 f5 43.♗d3 ♗xa4 44.♖xa4 ♗xc3

Here the game should have been adjourned, but Black resigned.

The second training match
At the beginning of November 1976, just four months after our training camp in Jurmala, I received another phone call from Tal. This time he invited me to come to Riga to play a short training match at the chess club there. He wanted to prepare for the upcoming USSR Championship in Moscow with a very strong line-up, which included Karpov [who would win convincingly. Tal finished 7th, Romanishin 9th -ed.]. Anyone who was at the club could come and watch, but as with the first match, the games were not published. And I was the only one who kept scoresheets. Tal was famously careless in such

matters, and I don't think he kept his.
In this second match, we played four games. In all of them Tal had a clear advantage, and I had to defend resourcefully. Tal's play was spectacular, but not quite reasonable enough, so he didn't win any of the games. Perhaps he was not really bothered...
In the final game, I managed to escape with a nice trick.

**Oleg Romanishin
Mikhail Tal**
Riga 1976 (match, 4)

position after 37.♖xa8

37...♗xf2
Tal thought this would be an easy win, but he had overlooked a neat detail.
He could have tried 37...♗c5!?, when it's impossible for White to attack the a2-pawn with his bishop. On the other hand, how should Black improve his position after 38.♖a6 ?
38.♔xf2 ♖h1

And Black wins, doesn't he? Well, not after **39.♗d1!** An amusing riposte, and suddenly White is really defending. **39...♖xd1** And draw agreed. ∎

What to watch for in Armageddon

Frowned upon and dismissed as fairly ludicrous not that long ago, Armageddon games have rapidly become commonplace tiebreakers. MAXIM DLUGY provides useful tips and tricks how to play them.

A rmageddon! The brutal search for a winner! When I hear this fearsome word, instead of shivering with bad premonitions or envisioning scenes from the Sistine Chapel, I get excited! There is always something magical in knowing that a contest that you've been watching for days or weeks – or only hours in the case of Norway Chess – will finally be decided in the space of minutes. No matter what.

First, for those who are less familiar with the phenomenon, let's look at the nature of an Armageddon game. The idea is to determine a winner in one single exciting game, in which both sides have to yield something. First the players toss to determine who can pick the colour they want to play – as White or as Black. The advantage of White is that you get more time, the disadvantage is that you have to win, since Black has draw odds. Black not only wins if he or she wins, but also if the game is drawn! A possible time-control is White getting five minutes against Black four, and a 1-second increment from move 61 onwards.

This year in Norway, the time-control was 10 minutes for White and 7 minutes for Black, with a 1-second increment starting from move 41. These differences for both sides create an interesting dynamic, and depending on their styles, they may have a clear preference for playing as White or Black.

Armageddon begins

Armageddon deciders have become popular only recently, but in fact they've been around for a while, even though I don't know when exactly they were first introduced. From my own experience I remember that in

1993, Bob Rice, a New York attorney who founded the Wallstreet Chess Club and later became the head of the Professional Chess Association, organized blitz tournaments in his office. This was near my workplace, and I loved to go there and play blitz, especially as some really strong players would compete in these events. One day I arrived and found my old friend Vishy Anand playing in a knock-out tournament. After two games, tied at 1-1, we found out that the tiebreaker would be an Armageddon game. My first Armageddon game ever! Anand picked Black and

although I actually came quite close to breaking down Vishy's stellar defences, he prevailed.

Maxim Dlugy
Vishy Anand
New York Wall Street 1993
Slav Defence

1.d4 d5 2.♘f3 ♘f6 3.c4 c6
During the normal match-up Vishy had lost with his favourite Grünfeld Defence. Just needing a draw, he opts for a much more solid set-up.
4.♕b3 dxc4 5.♕xc4 ♗f5 6.g3 e6 7.♗g2 ♘bd7 8.0-0 ♗e7 9.♘c3 0-0 10.e3

A contest that you've been watching for days or weeks will finally be decided in the space of minutes

This used to be one of my main weapons against the Slav, though later on I modified it by first playing 9.e3 and 10.♖d1, preserving the development of the b1-knight for later.

10...♘e4 11.♕e2 ♖c8 12.♘d2 ♘xd2 13.♗xd2

13...♗g6?! Somewhat passive. 13...e5 looks like a better attempt at equalizing, but Vishy's concept is to play fast and preserve time for thought for the later stages of the game. We will see how this strategy worked for him in this game.

14.e4 ♘f6 15.♗e3 ♗b4 16.f3 c5 17.♖fd1 cxd4 18.♗xd4

18...♕e7?! Somewhat dubious. The trade of the a-pawn for the c-pawn will be in my favour, as I will be getting a target on b7 and the two bishops to work on it.

18...♕a5 was better, though White still has an edge thanks to his control of the d-file and the passive bishop on g6.

19.♗xa7 ♗xc3 20.bxc3 ♖xc3 21.♗d4 ♖c6 22.♖ab1 22.♖ac1, trading one set of rooks, was more precise. **22...♖fc8 23.♕b5 ♖6c7 24.a4 h6 25.a5 ♔h7**

Typical Vishyism: He understands that for me to win the b-pawn I will have to open up the first rank. Therefore he is tucking away his king as far as possible, so that his counterplay will have effect without any checks from my side.

26.h4!?

26.♕b4 was a very strong idea, but I was loath to trade the queens.

In fact, Black can now make use of his strange-looking previous move and play: 26...♘g8!, rerouting the knight back into the game in case I trade the queens. Still, after 27.♕xe7 followed by 28.♗f1, White's advantage is quite significant.

26...h5 27.♔h2

27.♕b4 was even stronger now.

27...♘d7 28.♖d2 ♘c5 29.♗e5 ♖c6 30.♖bd1 ♕e8

31.♗f4? The player who wants to win should be looking for moves that go forward. In this position, after 31.♗d6!, threatening e5 and f4, Black would be in serious trouble.

31...♖a6 32.♖b2?

And now my time management caught up with me and I blundered into a simplification tactic. Correct was 32.♖b1, with a sizable advantage.

Vishy Anand has always been synonymous with ultra-fast thinking and decision-making.

32...♘a4! Anand is known for finding saving tactics in under a second. With this, Black has fully equalized, and I quickly start losing interest in the remainder of the game, as winning no longer seems possible.

33.♕xe8 ♖xe8 34.♖xb7 ♖xa5 35.♖a1 ♖aa8 36.♗e3 ♘c3 37.♖c1 ♖ac8 38.♗f1 ♘a4 39.♖a1 ♘c5 40.♖b5 ♘d7 41.♖d1 ♘f6 42.♖d2 ♖c3

43.♗g5? It's fully equal after 43.♖d3, but I had basically stopped looking. **43...♖xf3 44.♗e2 ♖f2+ 45.♔g1 ♘xe4** And I lost on move 55.

Anand's approach in this game was extremely practical: focus on the clock while keeping the position defensible. To keep the pressure up, I had to consume a lot of time, and this resulted in me failing to find some key moves during the critical moments of the game.

Raising the stakes

Although the World Chess Championship can now in fact be decided by an Armageddon game, according to FIDE's rules, the two most recent matches didn't go that far. Both against Karjakin in New York in 2016 and against Caruana in London in 2018, Magnus Carlsen finished off his formidable opponents in rapid play. However, at the FIDE World Cup in 2017 in Tbilisi, the eventual winner of the tournament, Levon Aronian, reached the final by defeating Maxime Vachier-Lagrave in an Armageddon game.

**Levon Aronian
Maxime Vachier-Lagrave**
Tbilisi World Cup 2017 (6.9)
London System

1.d4 ♘f6 2.♘f3 g6 3.♗f4 ♗g7 4.♘c3 d5 An interesting way to play against the London System.
5.♘b5 ♘a6 6.e3 0-0 7.h3 c6 8.♘c3 ♘c7 9.♗e2

9...b6 Earlier in their mini-match, Vachier-Lagrave chose 9...♗f5 and lost. This move is reasonable, but

slightly weakening. As a practitioner of the London, I would be more worried about the repositioning of the awkward knight from c7 to d6 via e8, although even then Black is still in need of a concrete plan to neutralize White's slight pull.
10.0-0 ♗b7 11.♗h2 c5 12.a4 a5 13.♘e5 An interesting positional concept to avoid trades would be 13.♘b5, followed by c3 and ♘a3.
13...♘d7 14.♘xd7 ♕xd7 15.♗g4 e6 16.♕d2 ♗c6 The opening did not go well for White, who needs to win; but now, let's see how masterfully Aronian extracts all the chances from this tedious position.
17.b3 ♖fc8 18.♘e2 cxd4

19.♘xd4 19.exd4 would be objectively better, but Aronian tries to complicate, even at the cost of worsening his position.
19...b5 20.axb5 ♘xb5 21.c3 ♘xd4 22.exd4 After 22.cxd4 a4 White would have to trade the last queenside pawns, and the position would be too easy for Black to draw.
22...a4 23.b4! ♗b5 24.♖fc1 a3 25.♗e2

25...♕c6?!

Looking for too many simplifications. 25...♗xe2 26.♕xe2 ♗h6 27.♖c2 ♖c4 was much stronger, depriving White of any real counterplay.
26.♗xb5 ♕xb5 27.♗d6! This keeps the intrigue going. On c5, the bishop can do a good job helping the b-pawn when the time comes.
27...♖c6 28.♗c5 ♖ca6 29.♖a2 ♕c4 30.♕e2!
The correct time to offer a queen trade, which Black should refuse.

30...♕xe2 It was better to pry the position open with 30...e5 or to keep the queens with 30...♕b3, but Maxime is feeling the pressure. He knows that each trade brings him closer to a draw and refuses to take in the objective value of the pieces. His queen is clearly stronger than White's.
31.♖xe2 a2 32.♖a1 ♖a3 33.♖c2 ♗f8 34.♔f1 e5 34...♗xc5 35.dxc5 ♔f8 is fine for Black, but looks quite complex, so Maxime goes for a safer-looking continuation.
35.♗xf8 ♔xf8 36.dxe5 ♔e7 37.♔e2 ♔e6 38.f4 d4! A good move, empowering Black's king.
39.cxd4

39...♔d5?

An inaccuracy. After the correct 39...♔f5! 40.d5 ♔xf4 41.e6 fxe6 42.dxe6 ♔e5 43.e7 ♔d6 Black runs down the pawn, with a draw in sight.
40.♖d2

Only moments before the all-decisive Armageddon game in the Tbilisi World Cup, Levon Aronian and Maxime Vachier-Lagrave kept making jokes.

40...♔c4? Finally, Levon gets his blunder. With seconds left on the clock, it's hard to choose the correct king route. Should Black go to support his a-pawn or try knocking off White's kingside pawns?

After 40...♔e4! 41.d5 ♔xf4 42.e6 fxe6 43.d6 ♖d8 44.♖axa2 ♖xa2 45.♖xa2 ♖xd6 46.b5 ♖b6 47.♖b2 ♔e4 the position would be drawn.

41.d5 ♔xb4 42.d6 ♔b3 43.♔f3
Black's problem is that his king is close but cannot really help the a-pawn.

43...♔c3 44.♖f2 h5

45.♔g3! Levon finds this nice manoeuvre for his king to get to f6. Black is lost.

45...♔d4+ 46.♔h4 ♔d5 47.♔g5?
This seemingly obvious move is actually a serious mistake. The correct idea was to use the d-pawn to create decisive threats. White's king position will decide later.

After 47.d7! ♔e6 48.♖fxa2 ♖xa2 49.♖xa2 ♖d8 50.♖a6+ ♔e7 51.♖d6

Black cannot go for the king and pawn ending and is lost.
47...♔e6 48.g4 hxg4 49.hxg4 ♖3a5
Black defended perfectly, and amazingly enough, the position is no longer a win for White. Therefore, the clock becomes the master of ceremonies.
50.♖e2 f6+! 51.♔xg6 ♖g8+ 52.♔h6 ♖xg4 53.f5+!

Once again, Aronian finds the murkiest line for Black to navigate, creating two connected passed pawns, while seemingly putting his king in danger. Still, when a draw is no good, risky play is the logical choice.
53...♔xf5 54.e6 ♖a8?
With so little time left on the clock, it's absolutely understandable that

Maxime did not find the only move to save the game. Check your intuition and give yourself a minute or two. What move would you play?
54...♖aa4!! is the only move, setting up a drawing mechanism. Now, if White plays 55.e7, 55...♖g6+ 56.♔h5 ♖g5+ 57.♔h6 ♖h4 is mate, so White must give up one of his passed pawns, which will result in a draw.
55.♖f1+ Now this wins. **55...♖f4 56.♖xf4+ ♔xf4 57.♖xa2 ♖xa2 58.e7 ♖d2 59.e8♕ ♖xd6 60.♕e7**

60...♖d4
To avoid losing his rook, Black has to give up the pawn immediately (check for yourself!).
61.♕xf6+
Defending this ending is trickier than winning it, and Aronian wins it handily.

61...♔e3 62.♔g5 ♖d5+ 63.♔g4
♖d4+ 64.♔g3 ♖d3 65.♕e5+
♔d2+ 66.♔f2 ♔c2 67.♕c5+
♖c3 68.♕f5+ ♔b2 69.♔e2
♖c2+ 70.♔d3 ♖c3+ 71.♔d2 ♖b3
72.♕e5+ ♔b1 73.♕d4

73...♖h3?
As said, it's more difficult to defend this endgame than to win it.
**74.♕b6+ ♔a1 75.♕f6+ ♔a2
76.♕e6+ ♖b3 77.♔c2 ♔a1**

Trying for one last trap, stalemate. But this was not Maxime's day.
78.♕a6+
Black resigned.

As we saw in this game, one of the key ways of playing Armageddon games for White is to continuously look for winning chances, while ignoring the objective assessment of the position. You basically have to eliminate all drawing continuations and play the best line that comes after that. In that case, you may get lucky, as Levon Aronian did in this game. Just remember, your opponent will probably make the mistake of looking for drawish continuations instead of exploiting your dubious moves.

King of Armageddon

No Armageddon story would be complete without an example from the World Champion of tie-breaks, Magnus Carlsen! In the following game, played in Norway Chess last year, Magnus seemingly effortlessly piles up pressure to break through a well-constructed pawn barrier to bag the point.

Magnus Carlsen
Vishy Anand
Stavanger 2019 Armageddon (1)
English Opening
1.c4 e5 2.♘c3 ♗b4 3.♘d5 ♗e7

This strange-looking line is a favourite of Anand and Alexei Shirov and shows their preference for knights over bishops. In faster time-controls, by the way, the knights are indeed more tricky to deal with, and averting their threats can cost valuable seconds on the clock.

4.d4 exd4
Vishy Anand prefers this continuation, while Shirov invariably chooses 4...d6. It's a matter of taste.
**5.♕xd4 ♘f6 6.♘xe7 ♕xe7
7.♗g5 ♘c6**

8.♕c3 The only real way to play for an advantage as 8.♗xf6 ♘xd4 9.♗xe7 ♔xe7 10.♖d1 doesn't promise much.
**8...♘e5 9.♘f3 d6 10.e3 h6
11.♗h4 g5**

12.♘xe5!? Not the most accurate move from the World Champion, but it seems he did not consider 12.♗g3 ♘e4 13.♕d4 ♘xg3 14.hxg3 c5! 15.♕e4 ♘xf3+ 16.♕xf3 ♗e6 complicated enough to outplay Anand.
12...dxe5? Vishy does not stop to think and misses a great retort. After the surprising intermezzo 12...♘e4! 13.♘g6! ♘xc3 14.♘xe7 ♔xe7 15.♗xg5+ hxg5 16.bxc3 g4! Black is hardly at risk of losing.
13.♗g3 ♘d7 14.h4 g4

Suddenly Black's position looks extremely suspect. White has two bishops, and Black's pawns expose his kingside. Analysing the opening part, we can conclude that Magnus Carlsen finds lines in which one inaccuracy can land his opponent in very serious problems, while the best move will lead to equality. Recently, several of the world's elite, when asked about the best prepared player in the world as regards the opening, all named

Magnus without the slightest hesitation. His secret lies in seeming to be unprepared, while actually hiding an amazingly deep understanding of the positions he plays in the back of his head.

15.c5?!

It's not quite clear why Magnus felt he needed to block Black's ...c5. After the natural 15.♗e2 h5 16.0-0 c5 17.f4! White would blow up Black's kingside and central positions, highlighting the weakness of Black's king.

15...h5 16.♖c1 c6 17.♗d3 0-0 18.0-0

With this move Magnus clearly shows his intention of slowly outplaying his opponent instead of going for the strong but complicated plan with 18.f3. It's an interesting trait of Magnus – if he knows he is better, he does not rush to crush his opponent, but relies on his superb technique to eventually outplay them. In this way he always has the situation firmly under control and is able to play his moves faster than his opponents, gradually increasing his time advantage and winning odds.

18...♖e8 19.♖fd1 ♘f6 20.♗b1 ♘d5 21.♕c2 e4 22.♖d4 f5

Magnus Carlsen finds lines in which one inaccuracy can land his opponents in very serious problems, while the best move will lead to equality

Black has accomplished a lot in the last few moves, creating what looks like an impregnable blockade in the centre and on the kingside. This makes White's win even more impressive.

23.a3 ♗e6 24.♖cd1 ♖ad8 25.♗a2 ♖d7 26.b4 a6 27.a4 ♖ed8 28.b5 axb5 29.axb5

29...♘f6?

It's strange that Anand felt compelled to do something in a position in which he just needed to sit tight on his blockade, which he destroys with this move.

After 29...♔f7 30.♖a4 ♕f6 31.bxc6 bxc6 32.♖dd4 ♔g7 33.♗d6 ♕xh4 White could go for 34.♗xd5 ♗xd5 35.♖xd5 cxd5 36.♗e5+ ♔f7 37.c6 ♖c8 38.♖a6, with a nearly decisive attack, while otherwise White would eventually strengthen the pressure against the c-pawn. It would be great to see how that game would have gone!

30.♖d6! With the invasive rook on d6, Vishy's position falls apart like a house of cards.

30...♗xa2 31.♕xa2+ ♕f7 32.♕a5 ♖xd6 33.cxd6

All Black's weaknesses, including the f5-pawn, are suddenly there for everyone to see. Black is lost.

33...♕d7 34.bxc6 bxc6 35.♖b1!

With the major pieces busy with the d6-pawn, Magnus redeploys his rook for invasion, threatening ♖b7 now.

35...♖f8 36.♕c7 ♖f7 37.♖b8+ ♔h7 38.♗e5 ♘d5 39.♖h8+ ♔g6 40.♕b8

Starting with 36.♕c7, White has moved his entire army up the board and now he finishes Black off on the eighth rank.

40...♘f6 41.♗xf6 ♔xf6 42.♖h6+ ♔e5

43.♕h8+

Black resigned. 43.♕b2 was mate in two, but Magnus couldn't be bothered.

Summing up: Magnus Carlsen managed to trick Vishy Anand in the opening, when the latter missed a nice intermediate move. He then chose to play a less complicated line instead of the stronger-looking aggressive continuation, but in doing so was able to put serious time-pressure on Vishy, who needed to figure out how to concoct a defence. With the time-pressure mounting, and Vishy realizing that he would be pressed for a long time, he decided to simplify and trade bishops, only to miss the decisive invasion of White's rook. Game Over!

Attackers vs Defenders: What is the best Armageddon strategy?

While thinking about Armageddon strategies, it dawned on me that players with an aggressive style are actually less likely to win Armageddons and should use their skills prior to getting there. The reasoning is simple: If you are a great defender and you win the toss, you will pick Black and be a serious favourite to win the match. If you lose the toss, your opponent may still pick White some 30-40 percent of the time, giving you an additional advantage again. An aggressive player who plays for a win with both colours, e.g. Baadur Jobava, would be at a disadvantage: he will not get the extra leverage from winning with Black, but the risks he usually takes in the openings to get a double-edged position would weigh against him when his opponent is in a must-win situation playing the white pieces.

To make a long story short, this factor is precisely what makes Magnus Carlsen such an amazing Armageddon player. His excellent defensive skills and the trademark pressure he gets with White make him nearly unstoppable in this kind of format.

In this year's Altibox Norway Chess, Fabiano Caruana was struggling mid-point, but managed to take down young Alireza Firouzja with this typical Armageddon play for White. Watch what Fabi does in the opening to extend his 10-7 time-lead straight out of the gate.

Fabiano Caruana
Alireza Firouzja
Stavanger 2020 (8, Armageddon)
Caro-Kann Defence, Fantasy Variation

1.e4 c6 2.d4 d5 3.f3

The so-called Fantasy Variation is an excellent choice with White against the Caro-Kann, especially when you have a 10-7 time-lead at the start of the game, as was the case in Norway Chess this time.

3...g6

Alireza Firouzja had played 3...dxe4, followed by 4...e5, against Caruana in their classical game earlier in the day, and had played the traditionally 'best' 3...♛b6 against Wei Yi in the summer. He must have studied this line quite a bit and understands that there is no clear-cut way to get a simple position here. His choice, based on playing it safe, looks good at first, but Fabiano shows that there are some problems with this as well.

4.♘c3 ♗g7 5.e5!

Once again, Fabiano makes the strongest move under the circumstances. The most common move, 5.♗e3, was undoubtedly what Alireza had analysed, and now he is forced to think for himself.

5...c5

It's very natural to undermine White's centre, but it is exactly here that White has prepared a nasty positional surprise.

It was more prudent to undermine White's centre from the other side. After 5...f6 6.f4 ♘h6 7.♘f3 ♗g4 8.♗e2 0-0 9.0-0 e6 Black should eventually equalize, after contesting the e5-square with his knights.

6.f4 cxd4 7.♛xd4 ♗e6 8.♘f3 ♘c6 9.♗b5 ♘h6 10.♗xc6+ bxc6 11.♛c5

A critical position has been reached. Black should be OK if he ignores some ghosts and plays direct chess. But it is precisely here that Alireza shows he had not really studied the position.

11...♗d7?!

Black should not retreat if he doesn't have to.

After the correct 11...♛b6 12.♘a4 ♛a6 13.b3 ♗g4 14.♘d4 ♘f5! 15.♛xc6+ ♛xc6 16.♘xc6 ♖c8 17.♘b4 f6! Black stands well.

It is difficult, of course, to decide on such aggressive play in this time-control. Now White gains an advantage.

12.♗e3 e6?

This very strange move is hard to explain. Black should simply have castled, of course, even with a worse position. Now he will have to give up a pawn to castle.

13.♘a4 ♘f5 14.♗f2 h5 15.♛c3!

White's bind on the dark squares is nearly decisive. Black makes the

Players with an aggressive style are actually less likely to win Armageddons and should use their skills prior to getting there

right decision to give himself some breathing space:

15...c5!? 16.♘xc5 0-0 17.0-0 ♗b5 18.♖fe1 ♕e7 19.a4 ♗c6 20.b4 ♖fc8 21.♕d2 ♗e8 22.c3 a5 23.h3 ♗f8 24.♔h2

White is not in a hurry, and slowly builds an unstoppable kingside attack.

24...♕c7 25.g4 ♘g7 26.♖g1 axb4 27.cxb4 d4 28.♗xd4 ♖d8 29.♘e4 ♗c6 30.♖ac1 ♕b7 31.♘f6+ ♔h8 32.f5 ♘e8

33.fxg6!

When you are winning in a blitz game, it is extremely important to focus on one tactical line and see it to the end. Fabiano does just that, without being scared to sacrifice material if necessary.

33...♗xf3 34.gxh5

34...fxg6?!

A tougher test of White's tactics was 34...♘xf6, when White should win after 35.exf6 ♔g8!! 36.♕g5! ♗d6+ 37.♗e5 ♗xe5+ 38.♕xe5 ♖d2+ 39.♔g3 ♖ad8 40.♖c7 ♕b6 41.♕c5! ♕xc5 42.♖xc5 ♘d3 43.♔f4, though this is not the kind of thing players analyse. When defending a tough position and needing only a draw, being able to find defensive resources like 35...♔g8 could go a long way towards making you an Armageddon powerhouse.

35.hxg6

Now there is no reasonable defence left.

35...♗g7 36.♕f4! ♖xd4 37.♕xd4 ♗h6 38.♕h4 ♕g7 39.♖cf1 ♗e2 40.♖f2 ♗d3 41.♘g4 ♗xg6 42.♘xh6 ♕xe5+ 43.♖g3 ♕h5 44.♕xh5 ♗xh5 45.♖f8+ ♔h7 46.♘f7 ♗xf7 47.♖xf7+ ♔h6 48.♖f8 ♔h7 49.♖gg8

Black resigned.

Summing up

To be a Master of Armageddon as White, one needs to:

1. Go forward whenever possible.

2. Try to surprise one's opponent in the opening.

3. Avoid all drawish lines, even at the expense of your position.

4. Keep up the pressure to draw down your opponent's time.

5. Display excellent positional understanding, so you will be able to quickly find solid moves that will continue to improve your position.

With Black one needs to:

1. Play briskly in the opening, creating a defensible position.

2. Play objectively for as long as possible, without being scared of dynamic play.

3. Concentrate on time management, since White will be spending time looking for winning chances.

4. Look for lines that could force significant simplification and drawish endgames.

Armed with these weapons, you can now start tying your matches and look forward to crushing your opponents in the Armageddon! ∎

MAXIMize
your Tactics
with Maxim Notkin

Find the best move in the positions below

Solutions on page 93

1. White to play

2. Black to play

3. White to play

4. White to play

5. White to play

6. White to play

7. Black to play

8. Black to play

9. White to play

GIBRALTAR

CONGRATULATIONS

TO WORLD CHAMPION

Magnus Carlsen &
The Play Magnus Group

For promoting chess to a wider global audience and for leading the monetisation of the game, which we believe to be for the benefit of all.

Chapeau, Magnus!

chess@caletahotel.gi
#gibchess

Photo Credit: David Llada

Judit Polgar

Aronian's lessons

Levon Aronian is not only one of the strongest GMs around, he's also one of the most interesting personalities on the circuit. **JUDIT POLGAR** looks at the qualities that make the Armenian special.

By the time I first actually met Levon Aronian during the 2001 European Championship in Ohrid, my trainer Lev Psakhis and others had already told me that he was a very promising talent. A few years later, Levon started visiting me at my place in Budapest. We spent many pleasant hours analysing together, but also had long conversations. I discovered that he had a well-rounded and colourful personality, with a strong and original sense of irony and humour but also with considerable intelligence. Those knowing Levon will agree that he is one of the most interesting characters in today's world chess elite.

I only played eight games against Aronian (including three blitz games), and feel proud to have a solid plus score against him. However, through the years I was always impressed when I followed his games, as they showed his sharp vision, deep understanding and an inexhaustible ability to find ambitious new opening ideas.

Levon Aronian's chess strength and leadership helped Armenia win the Chess Olympiad on three occasions. I would put him on a level with Kortchnoi and Bronstein, because I have always felt that he was destined to play a world title match.

Trademark 1: Slow growth. Those warning me about Aronian's talent must have seen deeper than his formal results. When we played our first game, he was aged 19 and his rating was 2528. Moreover, he failed to put up resistance in the crucial phase of the game.

Judit Polgar
Levon Aronian
Ohrid 2001

position after 33...♔g8

I have a symbolic advantage, due to my safer king and the possibility of

creating an outside passed pawn. With a minimum of care, Black should hold the draw.

34.♕d3 ♕e6?!

A strange decision, allowing me to continue to enjoy the favourable elements mentioned above.

34...♕xd3 35.♖xd3 ♖a8 would have neutralized them both, leading to a probable draw. I assume that Aronian, whose king was more vulnerable than mine, lost his sense of danger and objectivity.

35.a4 bxa4 36.bxa4

I now have chances to combine

I would put Aronian on a level with Kortchnoi and Bronstein, because I have always felt that he was destined to play a world title match

the threats on both wings, but still needed a little help from Black to make this plan come true.

36...♕c8?

After this passive move I doubt that Black will be able to save the game. Both 36...c5 and 36...♕e4 were more active, with reasonable chances to gradually equalize.

37.a5 ♕c7 38.♕d2!?

I do not understand why I did not take the pawn with 38.♕xf5. My last move defends both attacked pawns and prepares the decisive regrouping.

38...♖e7 39.a6 ♔g7 40.♖b3!

Threatening ♖b7.

40...♕a7 The only reasonable way to parry the threat, even if only temporarily. With the f4-pawn no longer under attack, my queen switches to the b-file.

41.♕b2+

Judit Polgar and Levon Aronian have a friendly chat at the start of their game at the 2012 London Chess Classic, a Marshall Attack that ended in a draw after 34 moves.

41...♔h6

Reminiscent of one of Kortchnoi's favourite moves as White, ♔g2-h3. The king is relatively safe on h6, but fails to defend against the attack on the seventh rank.

True, 41...♔f7 42.♕h8 would have yielded me a decisive attack.

42.♖b7 ♕e3 43.♖xe7 ♕xe7 44.♕b8 The optimal square for my queen. It supports the pawn's advance to the promotion square and defends f4, shattering any hopes of perpetual check. 1-0.

Two years later, Aronian was still on his way to the top, even though his rating had reached 2649 by now. In the next game, he again lost unnecessarily easily.

Judit Polgar
Levon Aronian
Hoogeveen 2003

position after 27.g3

My bishop pair is exerting annoying kingside pressure, and the central pawn requires permanent surveillance. Black's position is worse, but he would maintain drawing chances by sticking to a defensive policy. Instead, Aronian's next two pseudo-active moves ended in disaster.

27...♖c8?! It would have been better to defend the pawn with 27...♖b8.

28.♗d1 ♕c4??

A 'logical blunder', weakening the pressure on b5 and undermining the defence of my own pawn. Aronian missed a well-masked tactical idea.

29.♖c1!! Swedish GM Tom Wedberg commented: 'Judit never misses shots like this one.'

29...♕xc1

Sad necessity, as 29...♕xd3 30.♖xc8+ ♔h7 31.♗c2 would bring me an extra exchange and an easy win.

30.♗xc1 ♖xc1 31.d6 ♘d7 32.♔g2 Calmly preparing the final attack. 32...♗f6 33.♗c2 g6 34.♗b3 ♔g7 35.♕d5 1-0.

Trademark 2: A fighter. The painful lessons from his early years did not fail to have their effect. On his way to the top, Aronian developed the ability to turn the tables in desperate positions. In the next game, he achieved this with a move reminiscent of my 29.♖c1!! from the previous example.

Levon Aronian
Magnus Carlsen
London rapid 2019

Black has a consistent material advantage and the b-pawn is threatening. His king is a bit exposed, but this should not save White.

37.♖c1!? Forcing the queen to relinquish control of e6 and f7.

37...♕xc1 38.♕e8+ ♔h6 39.♕e6+

39...g6?

Instantly turning a won position into a lost one. It is interesting that Carlsen still had five minutes at this point.

39...♔g5?! would also lead to a draw after 40.♗e7+ ♔h5 41.♕f7+ ♔h6 42.♕e6+ ♔h5.

The only winning move was 39...♔h5!, not fearing any ghosts. Carlsen might have overlooked that after 40.♕f7+ g6 41.♕xh7+ he could defend with 41...♔h6. Indeed, taking the rook did not misplace the queen that badly. 42.♕e7 is ineffective: 42...♔g4!?, threatening ...♕h3+, followed by a back rank mate.

40.♗f8+ ♔h5 41.♕e7!

A 'quiet move' with a deadly double threat, ♕h4 mate and ♕xh7+, followed by mate. 1-0.

Trademark 3: Exquisite endgame technique and resourcefulness. In the vast majority of endgame positions, the truth is within human reach. However, sometimes it is so well-masked that the task can be anything but trivial over the board. The next game shows how Aronian excels in such situations. I could follow it first-hand, since I was the commentator at Norway Chess 2020, together with Vladimir Kramnik.

Jan-Krzysztof Duda
Levon Aronian
Stavanger 2020

A remarkable position. Without the pawn on a2, White would reach a draw, because his rook would have enough space to harass the black king along the a-file. Kramnik commented that the game would be drawn 'even without the a-pawn', but then I realized that the presence of this pawn did change the assessment!

50...♔e2! 51.♔g3

White needs to spend a tempo on this, since after 51.♖b6 ♖g4+ 52.♔h3 ♖g5 53.♖b2+ ♔f3 White is doomed in view of the poor placement of his king.

51...♖h7 52.♖b6

The attacks along the b-file are not effective, since the rook is too close to the black king. The a-pawn deprives the rook of a vital square, and White will be too late to clear enough space along the a-file.

52...e3 53.♖b2+ ♔d1 54.♖b1+ ♔c2 55.♖a1

Chess is the tragedy of one tempo... Indeed, with White to move, the endgame would be drawn after a2-a4 or... giving the pawn for a good cause.

55...♖f7 56.a4 Too late, unfortunately, since the e-pawn is ready to advance.

56...e2 57.♔g2 ♖f5 Playing for zugzwang. The more straightforward 57...♔d2 also wins: 58.♖a2+ ♔e3 59.♖a3+ ♔e4 60.♖a1 ♖d7, with the same idea as in the game.

58.♖a2+ ♔d3 59.♖a1 ♔e3 60.♖a3+ ♔e4 61.♖a1

61...♖d5! Threatening ...♖d1. 0-1. With the white pawn one step further, White would still draw with 62.♔f2 ♖d1 63.♖a4+ ♔d3 64.♖a3+ ♔d2 65.♖a2+.

An incredible performance by Aronian, who squeezed his chances out of a minor detail.

Conclusions

■ One should not be put off by a player's slow growth during his younger years. Slow can be equivalent with deep, if continually sustained by hard work.

■ The game is not over until the score sheets have been signed. It is essential to look for practical chances until the very last moment.

■ When evaluating and planning in the endgame, every tiny detail can make a big difference with respect to the known patterns. ■

1. Bodnaruk-Solozhenkina
Sochi 2020

With 29...♖c8 Black has created a target for a deadly blow: **30.♖xd5+!** **exd5 31.♕h3+** Taking back the rook and even winning the queen. Black resigned.

2. Martin Duque-Berkes
Spain tt 2020

34...♖c1! Now White can no longer defend the d-pawn. He played **35.♖xc1 ♗xd4** and soon resigned. On 35.♕f1, the most convincing is 35...♕xd4+ 36.♖xd4 ♗xd4+.

3. So-S.Zhigalko
chess.com 2020

20.♗h6+! Trick or treat! Which piece to take? 20...♔xf6 21.♕g5 is checkmate. Black chose **20...♖xh6** and White easily converted after **21.♘e8+ ♔h7 22.♘xc7**.

4. Murzin-Potkin
Sochi 2020

48.♖xg6+! ♔h7 After 48...fxg6 the white queen walks a long road to give mate: 49.♕d5+, 50.♕xe5+, 51.♕e6+, 52.♕h3+ and 53.♕h7 mate. **49.♖f6 ♕xe7 50.♕h3+ ♔g8 51.♕g3+** Black resigned.

5. Arvola-Skotheim
Fagernes 2020

White is first to check, but one of his following checks has to be very special: **52.♖h8+ ♔g7 53.♕g8+ ♔f6 54.♕xf7+!** Here it is! **54...♔xf7 55.♖b7+** Black resigned, as after 55...♔f6 he is checkmated by 56.♖f8.

6. Postny-Bakalchuk
Israel tt 2020

22.♖xd4! And Black resigned because each recapture has its flaws: 22...cxd4 leaves the queen en prise, after 22...♕xd4 23.♖d1 it falls into a trap, while 22...exd4 23.♗g3 drops a rook.

7. S. Zhigalko-Gelman
chess.com 2020

Two exchanges is not too high a price to get access to g2: **32...♖xe3!** **33.♘xe3 ♖xe3! 34.♖xe3** Or 34.fxe3 ♕xg2+ 35.♔e1 ♕e2 mate. **34...♕xg2+ 35.♔e1 ♕g1+ 36.♔d2 ♕d1** Mate.

8. Villegas-Karjakin
chess.com 2020

26...♖xb5! 27.axb5 ♖a2 Catching the white king in a mating net. 27...♖xc3+ 28.♖xc3 ♖a2 wins as well. **28.♕xb4** Or 28.♖hf1 ♘h2+ 29.♔e3 ♘xf1+, gaining material and mating all the same. **28...♖f2** Mate.

9. Kozul-Ristic
Slovenia tt 2020

23.♖xd7! ♖xd7 24.♗xb5! ♖xd6 If 24...♕xb5, 25.♖c8+ ♔g7 26.♕d4+ mates. 24...♕xd6 25.♖c8+ is similar to the game. **25.♖c8+ ♔g7 26.♕c3+ f6 27.♗xa6** And Black can't retake due to 28.♕c7+, mating.

Openings for everyone

If one of your New Year's resolutions was to work on your openings, **MATTHEW SADLER** is happy to be your guide. No matter if you're looking for safe and solid or unusual and adventurous.

The past year has truly been the year Britain upped its hyperbole game. In common with many, I count 2020 as one of the lesser years of my life ('so far' pointed out an optimistic friend), yet here in the UK, our government has provided the events of the year with an incessant accompaniment of heady rhetoric. However, just when you think you've finally become desensitised to it all – I barely batted an eyelid this morning when our Prime Minister hailed the 'wonderful' new post-Brexit customs forms – something comes along that punches through those barriers of indifference. I am talking, of course, about Rustam Kasimdzhanov's claim that the *Benoni is back in business* (ChessBase DVD).

Treebeard's cry 'A wizard should know better!' (*Lord of the Rings*) was the phrase that popped into my head when I saw this title, but indeed Kasimdzhanov does know better. This is a companion course to Kasimdzhanov's earlier ChessBase DVD on the Nimzo-Indian (1.d4 ♘f6 2.c4 e6 3.♘c3 ♗b4) and recommends the Modern Benoni only against the third moves 3.♘f3 and 3.g3. In this way, the most dangerous attacking varia-

tions – particularly the 'Flick Knife' attack as John Doknjas calls the variation after 3.♘c3 c5 4.d5 exd5 5.cxd5 d6 6.e4 g6 7.f4 ♗g7 8.♗b5+ in *The Modern Benoni* (Everyman Chess) – are sidestepped. White's remaining possibilities are still challenging but at least Black's king is never in immediate danger. However, if you are looking to only play the Modern Benoni against 1.d4, you need to look a little further than this DVD – for example to John Doknjas's book.

The DVD format has plusses and minuses compared to learning from a book. The biggest minus is the time it takes to go through complicated variations, which tends to make DVD repertoires less detailed than book repertoires. On the other hand, the DVD presenter can flag key variations and important moves more effectively to the viewer than is possible in a book, which in theory should make the essentials of an opening easier to learn. ChessBase also offers a couple of interesting

features such as Repertoire Training (to drill your openings by replaying them) and Practice Positions (where you get the chance to play out positions from the DVD against an engine of your chosen strength). I confess that the first feature didn't work for me – after clicking any of the provided links, I just got sent to the starting position, with no clear indication of what I was supposed to do. The Practice Positions feature did work however, and I was soon happily taking club player level Fritz's pawns and pieces, although getting hold of the game afterwards seemed unnecessarily difficult (I didn't manage – the download button only gave me garbled output).

The meat of the DVD, however, is the presentation of the recommended lines. Former FIDE World Champion and current Caruana coach Rustam Kasimdzhanov starts off with a presentation of famous Modern Benoni games (from Nimzowitsch-Marshall, New York 1927, to the Leko-Kramnik World Championship match in 2004) and then takes us through five chapters of variations.

I thought the DVD started excellently as I greatly enjoyed the model games and I also felt that Kasimdzhanov did a super job of explaining the modern main line 1.d4 ♘f6 2.c4 e6 3.♘f3 c5 4.d5 d6 5.♘c3 exd5 6.cxd5 g6 7.h3 ♗g7 8.e4 0-0 9.♗d3.

He also does an interesting section on 9.♗e3 and 9.♗g5, which had never occurred to me before and which are also not covered in Doknjas's book. However, I confess to getting rather confused during the explanation of the classical main line 1.d4 ♘f6 2.c4 e6 3.♘f3 c5 4.d5 d6 5.♘c3 exd5 6.cxd5 g6 7.♘d2 ♗g7 8.e4 0-0 9.♗e2. These are extremely tricky. After castling, White has moves such as a4, ♖a3,

Treebeard's cry 'A wizard should know better!' was the phrase that popped into my head when I saw this title

The Benoni is back in business
Rustam Kasimdzhanov
FritzTrainer Opening
ChessBase DVD, 2020
★★★☆☆

The Modern Benoni
John Doknjas
Everyman Chess, 2020
★★★☆☆

♕c2, h3 and ♖e1 which he can throw in at various stages (he can even do some of them before castling) and the move orders make some difference, if I understand Kasimdzhanov correctly. However, even taking notes, I did not get much closer to grasping the differences. It felt to me as if Kasimdzhanov had more affinity with the White side than with the Black side and that he was finding it hard to become too enthusiastic about Black's prospects. Kasimdzhanov's comment 'We seem to be all right ...

Kasimdzhanov could certainly learn something about sales technique from Boris Johnson!

give or take' at the end of the video on the line 9...♖e8 10.0-0 ♘bd7 11.♕c2 ♘e5 made me feel he could certainly learn something about sales technique from Boris Johnson! I think this influenced me slightly for the rest of the video, as I didn't enjoy that as much as the first excellent chapters.

In such cases, my feeling is that you need a blend of materials to learn the opening, and an excellent candidate for this additional material is John Doknjas's already mentioned Everyman book. The author is a young Canadian FM and was unknown to me before I read this book. I tend to be suspicious when players of this strength write large opening books, but, keeping an open mind this time, I think he's done an excellent job!

Firstly, he agrees with a lot of Kasimdzhanov's repertoire choices, which makes using both at the same time extremely valuable: there's much more detail in Doknjas's 440+ page book and it's easier to look back quickly for a variation in a book than in a DVD. Secondly, the book fills

in gaps in any sidelines that Kasimdzhanov skims over, as well as all the lines arising after 3.♘c3 c5. Thirdly, Everyman really does produce clear, good-looking books that are a pleasure to read, with big print and plenty of diagrams.

All in all, with the DVD and this book together I felt I had a complete body of Modern Benoni knowledge to be getting on with! Both book and DVD are between 3 and 4 stars but as I am writing this it's still 2020, so to remain in character for the year, I'll give them a miserly 3! Together though, they make an excellent 4!

■ ■ ■

Unconventional Approaches to Modern Chess – Volume 1 by Alexander Ipatov (Thinkers Publishing) was a crazy ride through weird opening theory for Black, and Ipatov repeats the same feat with *Unconventional Approaches to Modern Chess – Volume 2*, but this time for the White side! The book is divided up into three parts. Part 1 proposes some sidelines in mainstream openings such as the Queen's Gambit Declined, the Slav, the Catalan and the Grünfeld. Part 2 looks at typical setups practised by the creative players Mamedyarov and Jobava. Finally, Part 3 gets a bit wilder still, with crazy ideas in lines like 1.b3 and even the Open Sicilian!

It is a tremendous outpouring of creativity and a great exposition of the ideas and analysis strong modern grandmasters can produce. The very first chapter had me laughing with pleasure as Ipatov demonstrated his

sideline weapon against the Queen's Gambit Declined.
1.d4 ♘f6 2.c4 e6 3.♘f3 d5 4.♗g5

This system is a favourite of the always tricky English grandmaster Mark Hebden. My understanding was that White was hoping for a quiet game off the beaten paths after 4...♗e7 5.♘bd2. Ipatov's idea is quite different however!
4...♗e7 5.e3 0-0 6.♕c2
The first surprise. Why would White play the queen to c2 so early?
6...h6 7.♗xf6 ♗xf6 8.h4

This is Ipatov's idea. After struggling to demonstrate any advantage after the normal 8.♘c3 c5 9.dxc5 dxc4 10.♗xc4 ♕a5, Ipatov decided that the development of the queen's knight should be delayed because after **8...c5** Ipatov's idea is to play **9.g4**

Threatening a quick g5! What a great idea, combining a pawn storm that has been known for decades with ultra-modern move order subtleties.

The following chapters are just as stimulating, introducing a host of fresh ideas to the 4.g3 line against the Slav (1.d4 d5 2.c4 c6 3.♘f3 ♘f6 4.g3) and to the following pawn sacrifice against the Catalan: 1.d4 d5 2.c4 e6 3.♘f3 ♘f6 4.g3 ♗b4+ 5.♘bd2 dxc4 (instead of the normal and duller 5.♗d2).

Moving on to the English, Ipatov takes a good look at an unusual line that I first saw recommended by IM Lorin D'Costa and that is also put forward for White in the recent *Iron English* by Simon Williams and Richard Palliser (Everyman Chess).
1.c4 e5 2.g3 ♘f6 3.♗g2 d5 4.cxd5 ♘xd5 5.♘c3 ♘b6 6.e3 ♘c6 7.♘ge2

White avoids the well-worn main lines with 6.♘f3 and develops the knight flexibly to e2. A key White idea is to play the dark-squared bishop to b2 and then attack the e5-pawn with f4. Lorin D'Costa featured a great

Unconventional Approaches to Modern Chess Volume 2
Alexander Ipatov
Thinkers Publishing, 2020
★★★★★

game by Nakamura with this theme on his DVD.
7...♕d3 Interestingly, Stockfish and AlphaZero fought out some games in this line in 2018 with AlphaZero choosing maximum activity with 7...♕d3, with good positions for Black.
8.f4
'This is pretty much White's only idea in the position' according to Ipatov, but Stockfish came up with a few other interesting lines that I haven't seen anywhere else in over-the-board or correspondence databases: 8.a4

A feast of unusual ideas and probably a few surprise weapons you can use in your repertory as well

♗b4 9.♗e4 (9.f4 f6 10.♕b3 a5 11.fxe5 fxe5 12.0-0 ♗f5 13.g4 ♗g6 14.♕e6+ ♔d8 15.♗xc6 bxc6 16.♕xc6 ♖b8 17.♘g3 ♖f8 18.♖xf8+ ♗xf8 was a typical crazy mess for this line, with White a pawn up but still facing problems developing the queen-side pieces, Stockfish-AlphaZero, Computer Match 2018 (½-½, 256)) 9...♕d8 (9...♕a6 10.♘b5 is White's idea) 10.f4 a5 11.♕c2 f6 12.♘b5 ♗h3 13.fxe5 fxe5 14.♘g1 ♗g4 15.♗xc6+ bxc6 16.♕xc6+ ♔e7 17.♕e4 ♕d7 18.h3 ♗f5 19.♕xe5+ ♔d8 20.♘e2 ♖e8 21.♕d4 ♗d3 22.b3 c5 23.♕xd7+ ♔xd7, with two pawns' worth of mess in Stockfish-AlphaZero, Computer Match 2018 (½-½, 69).
8...f6 9.♗e4 ♕a6
Here Palliser and Williams recom-

mend 10.a3 as an interesting try, while Ipatov mentions 10.fxe5 fxe5 11.a3. In principle, I like Palliser and Williams's idea of keeping the option of f5 clamping down on the black kingside, though Black does get the opportunity to play ...f5 himself. The idea of a3 is simply to go after the black queen on a6!
10.a3 ♗g4 11.h3 ♗e6 12.♖b1 0-0-0 13.b4

Threatening b5! Black needs to be well-prepared for this!

A little later, Ipatov turns his attention to the combination of 1.b3 and ♖g1, such as:
1.b3 ♘f6 2.♗b2 e6 3.e3 c5 4.f4 b6 5.♘f3 ♗b7 6.♖g1

I think I've given you a good taster of the content! As you can see, it's both inspiration and preparation: a feast of unusual ideas and probably a few surprise weapons you can use in your repertory as well. I wasn't planning to award any 5 stars this month, but reading through the book again, I don't think I can avoid it! The openness and enthusiasm with which Ipatov shares ideas that must have cost him a great deal of effort and time to discover and analyse should be rewarded!

■ ■ ■

I mentioned *The Iron English* by Simon Williams and Richard Palliser (Everyman Chess) in the notes above. This book is a good exposition of an English repertoire based around the Botvinnik formation of pawns on c4 and e4 and the standard opening moves 1.c4, 2.♘c3, 3.g3, 4.♗g2, 5.e4 and 6.♘ge2. It leans heavily on Simon Williams's experience with this line (how often do you see games by GingerGM and Mikhail Botvinnik next to each other in a book?) and does a very complete job of covering all manner of move orders that Black can throw at White.

The book begins with an outline of key ideas for White and then an overview of the 'Iron English' repertory, which acts as an extremely useful reference point for the lines to come. Each new section also has a quick outline of the theory before the illustrative games start. I think these were important sections to add as I was struck while reading the book how many move orders White must contend with when playing the English, especially when you're looking for a specific structure like

**The Iron English
Simon Williams &
Richard Palliser
Everyman Chess,
2020**
★★★☆☆

the Botvinnik against as many lines as possible.

I tried hard to find some gaps, but I didn't find any. For example,
1.c4 c5 2.♘c3 ♘c6 3.g3 ♘f6 4.♗g2 e6 5.e4 d5

is a radical way for Black to attack the Botvinnik structure, which I'd looked at a couple of years ago, but we get four pages on this line, and the analysis matches my own (slight edge for White).
1.c4 e5 2.♘c3 ♘f6 3.g3 ♗c5

I thought for a long time that this idea had been missed, but I finally found the line buried in Theory Section 6E! There have been some very sharp games after 4.♗g2 c6 5.♘f3 e4 6.♘h4 d5 7.cxd5 cxd5 8.d3 ♘g4 9.0-0 g5, including some Stockfish-AlphaZero game covered on the Game Changer YouTube channel of Natasha Regan and me, but the authors suggest something much more sensible!
4.♘f3 Simple and sensible, transposing, after 4...d6 or 4...♘c6, to standard lines.

I suppose my only doubts about this book while reading it were related ironically to one of its strengths: its thoroughness! I would imagine that club players looking to take up this line would see it as a way of avoiding learning too much theory and yet here is a book of more than 450 pages! Moreover, as you can see from the second line above, it doesn't prove possible to play the Botvinnik setup against absolutely everything and there are a few lines which seem to me somewhat out of the comfort zone of the normal solid English player. However, once you have a reference work like this, it's up to you to pick out what you need and you always have a big body of knowledge to fall back on. Note that this book is also available as a Chessable course, so that might also appeal as a way of working through and drilling the variations in the book! For me this is again somewhere between 3 and 4 stars, but in the spirit of 2020, we'll stick with 3!

■ ■ ■

The Caro-Kann Revisited – A Complete Repertoire for Black, by Francesco Rambaldi (Thinkers Publishing), caught my eye when I got asked some questions about the Caro-Kann recently. The Italian Grandmaster Rambaldi, now living in the US, presents a thoroughly modern repertoire, meeting the Advance (1.e4 c6 2.d4 d5 3.e5) with the Khenkin-Arkell 3...c5, which is a nice change from the somewhat stale 3...♗f5 lines which have appeared in a lot of repertoire books, and the Classical 3.♘c3 with my countryman David Howell's beloved 3...dxe4 4.♘xe4 ♘f6.

1.e4 c6 2.d4 d5 3.♘c3 dxe4 4.♘xe4 ♘f6

which again is more exciting for Black than 4...♗f5 and less fraught than 4...♘d7 ! My current test for

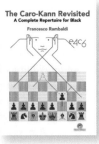

The Caro-Kann Revisited: A Complete Repertoire for Black
Francesco Rambaldi
Thinkers Publishing, 2020
★★★★☆

such books is how thoroughly the author deals with the 'boring' side-lines, such as the Exchange Variation (3.exd5 cxd5), and there once again Rambaldi finds a little-known move order (4.♗d3 ♘f6 5.c3 ♗g4) to inject some spice into this line.

It's a complicated grandmaster-level repertoire and thus not for a club player starting out with the Caro-Kann, but for existing Caro-Kann players looking for some deep analysis to supplement their own repertoire with, it's an excellent choice. I've already recommended it to someone, so I'll do the same to you! 4 stars!

■ ■ ■

Finally, from ultra-modern opening variations and subtle move orders we go all the way back to the mid-to-late 1800s and *Steinitz In London – A Chess Biography with 623 Games* by Tim Harding (McFarland). This is another beautifully produced hardback edition from McFarland and is a pleasure to read, as always. The story starts in earnest with Steinitz' arrival in London for the London Congress of 1862 and Harding traces casual games played by Steinitz against strong British players like Deacon, Burden and Bird. The tournament itself was the normal 19th century craziness, with games played at the players' discretion over a period of three weeks. Inevitably the tournament ended with players not having met each other and having played different numbers of games! However, England must have appealed to Steinitz, as he remained there for 20 years, building up his

Steinitz In London A Chess Biography with 623 Games
Tim Harding
McFarland, 2020
★★★★☆

reputation as the World's strongest player after defeating Anderssen 8-6 in 1866.

What hadn't occurred to me before reading the book was how little top-level chess the top players of that era played. Steinitz survived for many years on a diet of odds games, offhand games, and simultaneous displays, both normal and blindfold, with only the occasional tournament or higher-level match. I was to be honest somewhat disappointed in the quality of Steinitz' games during this period. I also felt that there was little discernible development in his chess: 20 years later he was still playing the same dubious King's Gambits, still missing some obvious tactics. There was the interesting tournament Vienna 1873 where he played 1.c4 in many games (and even 1.a3!), but looking at his games after that, he was soon back to the old ways. By contrast, his play at Hastings 1895, despite, at the age of 59, being past his peak, was much more varied and interesting. I think you really see the value there of his tumultuous World Championship matches against Zukertort, Chigorin and Lasker. Testing himself against such strong rivals in the most important event inevitably developed Steinitz' own game and unlocked his true potential.

However, this book is not all about the chess! We follow Steinitz as he marries, becomes a father, becomes a journalist and an author, quarrels bitterly with the English chess establishment, all beautifully documented and explained. Definitely a nice book for the dark evening hours with a glass of wine next to you! 4 stars! ■

They are The Champions

SEHYUN KWON
South Korea

The following fragment is from his game against Cherniaev, who challenges his much lower-rated opponent with the King's Gambit – a strategy that quickly backfires.

Alexander Cherniaev (2436)
Sehyun Kwon (2117)
London 2017
1.e4 e5 2.f4 exf4 3.♗c4 ♕h4+ 4.♔f1 d6 5.d4 ♗e6 6.♕d3 ♘d7 7.♘c3 ♘gf6 8.♘f3 ♕h6 9.♘b5 ♔d8 10.♘c3 ♘h5 11.♔f2 ♗e7 12.♖f1 ♔c8 13.♔g1

The new chess champion of South Korea is Candidate Master Sehyun Kwon. The championship was originally planned at the beginning of the year, but was postponed because of the pandemic. To reduce the risk of infection, the number of participants was limited to seven players. Besides the usual Covid-measures (masks, temperature checks, cleaning), the players wore gloves during play. The six-round tournament was held over a four-day period in Incheon at the end of November.

The first round turned out to be decisive, as Sehyun Kwon beat title favourite IM Hongjin Ahn with the black pieces. Sehyun Kwon continued to win, and after five rounds (5 out of 5!) he was already certain of the title.

Go is by far the most popular board game in Korea. Why did Sehyun choose chess over Go? Sehyun Kwon lived in South Africa from the age of 6 to 10 and became interested in chess after beating his friends and schoolteacher at the school chess club. After returning to Korea, he joined a local tournament and has been in love with chess's charm ever since. He enjoys thinking of strategies and tactics that can bring him victory. At the age of 22, he has already participated in two Chess Olympiads (Baku and Batumi) and two Youth World Chess Championships.

Yet, of all the tournaments, Sehyun Kwon's most memorable chess experience was the London Chess Classic in 2017, where he beat GM Alexander Cherniaev and GM Prasanna Vishnu. Sehyun needed a draw in the last round for an IM norm, but eventually lost against IM Anthony Bellaiche. He was obviously disappointed, but it did prove to him that he can compete with much higher-rated players.

White has 'manually castled', but his king is still not safe and Black's pawn storm ...g5/...f5 is coming. **13...g5 14.♘d5 ♗d8 15.♕c3 ♖g8 16.♗d2 ♕g6 17.♘d3 ♗xd5 18.exd5 f5 19.♖ae1 ♗g7 20.♔h1 ♘f6**

21.♘xg5 White sacrifices a piece for two pawns to stem Black's attack but it is not enough. **21...♕xg5 22.♗xf4 ♕g6 23.♗g3 ♘e4 24.♗xe4 fxe4 25.♖e2 ♘h5 26.♗e1 ♘f6 27.♕b3 ♕h5 28.♖d2 ♘g4 29.h3 e3 30.♖d3 ♘f2+ 31.♗xf2 ♕e2 32.♔g1 ♕f3 33.g4 exf2+ 34.♖xf2 ♕e4 35.♕c4 h5** And Black won (0-1, 50).

Sehyun Kwon is now a full-time chess professional who studies on his own, without a coach. Currently, he is working through Jacob Aagaard's *GM Preparation* series and uses the ChessKing software to improve.

Kwon participated in the Online Chess Olympiad, and he also takes part in the chess.com Titled Tuesday tournaments. His ambition is not only to become a better player himself, but also to inspire others to become better chess players. ∎

In **They are The Champions** we pay tribute to national champions across the globe. For suggestions please write to editors@newinchess.com.

Jan Timman

My favourites

The study database of Harold van der Heijden is an inexhaustible goldmine. On the occasion of the publication of the new enlarged version **JAN TIMMAN** presents study highlights from the past five years.

Harold van der Heijden is a man of unimaginable diligence and discipline. As a researcher in veterinary diagnostics, he quickly developed a blood test for minks. It was hectic work, made urgent by the various corona outbreaks in the mink farms during the Covid-19 pandemic. At the same time, Van der Heijden published a new version of his study database. It now contains 93,839 studies, over 8,000 more than the version of five years ago. A large number of old studies was dismantled in the process; the increasingly strong computers mercilessly exposed their weak spots.

For me, the new database was a goldmine, but this probably won't apply to every grandmaster. Four years ago, I spoke about studies with Anish Giri. He had also bought Van der Heijden's database, but was disappointed by what he had found there. It's true that it contains quite some mediocre studies. I advised Giri to concentrate on the First Prizes.

I must confess, however, that even this does not guarantee that the practical player would be impressed, the reason being that endgame study specialists use very different criteria when judging a study. When Judit Polgar and I look at studies, we like the same things: beautiful turns, spectacular moves, combinations and unexpected mating and stalemate patterns. The experts look for themes: they can appreciate moves that we shrug our shoulders over, thinking 'What else?' They also have a sharp eye for judging whether the various phases of a study form a seamless whole. The practical player, in contrast, likes to see variety, as in a game. Here is an example:

Jan Timman
2nd prize, Azerbaijan CCC-50
Anniversary Tourney 2020

The first move is clear: White must prevent the advance of the foremost g-pawn.

1.♖cc3 ♘b3! This knight move disrupts the coordination of the white rooks on the third rank.
2.♗xb3 Insufficient for the win was 2.♖xg3? in view of 2...♔xg3 3.♗xb3 g4 4.g7 ♗f3 5.g8♕ ♖xg8 6.♗xg8 ♔h2, and the tablebase indicates that White cannot win, despite his lead in material.
2...g2 3.♖h3+! A forced rook sacrifice. White is going to corner the black king.
3...♔xh3 4.♗e6+ ♔h2 5.♖h3+ ♔g1 6.g7 g4 Now White must choose the correct square for the rook.
7.♖h4!
It is very important to attack the hindmost black g-pawn. After 7.♖h8? ♖b1+ 8.♔xe2 ♖b2+ 9.♔e1 ♖b1+ White cannot escape the rook checks, as witness the following line: 10.♔d2 ♔f2 11.♖f8+ ♔g3 12.g8♕ ♖d1+! 13.♔c2 ♖c1+ 14.♔b2 ♖b1+ 15.♔a2 ♖a1+ 16.♔xa1 g1♕+ 17.♔a2 ♕a7+, and perpetual check.
7...g3 8.♗h3! An important move.
8...♖g8

9.♖h7 An interesting moment. A situation of reciprocal zugzwang has arisen. White to play would be unable to win.

9...♔h2 There is also a second, far shorter main line: 9...♖xg7 10.♖xg7 ♔h2 11.♖h7! g1♕+ 12.♗f1 mate.
10.♗e6+ ♔g1 11.♗xe2 White takes a time-out by taking the pawn. But now Black is going to aim for stalemate.

11...♖h8! A quite venomous riposte.
12.♖h3! It is of great importance that the white rook is protected. Insufficient was 12.♔f3? in view of 12...♖d8!, e.g. 13.♖h8 ♔f1 14.♗h3 ♖d3+ 15.♔f4 ♔f2 16.♗xg2 ♖d4+ 17.♔f5 ♖d5+! 18.♔f6 ♖d6+ 19.♔e7 ♖g6, with a draw.
12...♖e8
Black's chance, since after 12...♖xh3 13.♗xh3 ♔h2 14.♗xg2 the white pawn would queen.
13.♖h6 ♖g8
On 13...♖b8 White wins by 14.♗d5!, targeting the foremost black g-pawn.
14.♖g6
Now all stalemate attempts will be moot.

14...♔h2
A last-ditch attempt.
15.♗xg8! g1♕ 16.♖h6+ ♔g2 17.♗d5
The second bishop mate.

Harold van der Heijden's significantly enlarged database is a treasure trove for anyone who appreciates the beauty of studies.

The study tournament was held to celebrate the 50th anniversary of the Azerbaijan Chess Composing Commission, and was judged by problem and endgame study composer Muradkhan Muradov, who turned 70 recently. He was enthusiastic about my study, but not all the experts shared his feelings.

I often read the blog of the Ukrainian study composer Sergiy Didukh, which include posts by various prominent experts such as World Champion Oleg Pervakov. Didukh has a vast knowledge of endgame studies, especially from a historical point of view, and a sharp, often cutting pen. About my study

Van der Heijden's new study database contains 93,839 studies, over 8,000 more than the version of five years ago

he wrote: 'The first three moves spoil the starting position, and there is no particular sense in the sacrifices.'

That kind of surprised me. I was actually quite happy with the sacrifices from both sides. The study shouldn't start with a black pawn on g2, as the German grandmaster Jan Sprenger also observed in Didukh's blog. The mutual sacrifices are thematic, and the study starts with a combination and ends in subtle play in which White must continually avoid stalemates.

This study cannot be found in Van der Heijden's database, incidentally, because it is too recent. To give you a good idea of the high points of the past five years, I have put together a selection of studies. They are personal preferences, of course, and I have left out most complex studies.

I start with a study by 61-year-old Nikolay Ryabinin who, like Botvinnik at the time, is an electro-technician by trade. He was recently made a grandmaster (in the area of endgame studies). This study is one of the last from the previous database. I have included it because I find it so impressive.

Nikolay Ryabinin
1st prize, Fokin-90 Jubilee
Tourney 2015

White's first job is to stop the black h-pawn.
1.♖h5 g6+ The only way to create counterplay.
2.♔xg6 ♗e8+ 3.♔h7 The best square for the king. White is going to launch a mating attack.

3...♗xh5 4.♗h6+! Forcing the black king to a less favourable square. **4...♚e8 5.♗g5! ♚f8!** The only move. 5...h1♛ would have run into 6.d7+ ♚f8 7.e7+ ♚f7 8.e8♛ mate. **6.♗e7+!** The start of a subtle manoeuvre. The immediate 6.d7? wouldn't yield anything after 6...♗e8! 7.e7+ ♚f7 8.d8♞+ ♗xd8 9.exd8♛ h1♛+, with a draw. **6...♚e8**

7.♗h4!
This was the idea. White shields the

Pervakov's reply was stunning: 'From the age of 25, I have spent all my life composing studies'

h-file before advancing his d-pawn.
7...♚f8 8.d7 ♗d8! An ingenious defence. The alternative 8...♗e8 was insufficient in view of 9.e7+ ♚f7 10.d8♞+ (not 10.d8♛?, in view of 10...h1♛) 10...♗xd8 11.exd8♛ h1♛ 12.♛e7 mate.
9.♗xd8 ♗e8! Black goes all-out to prevent mate. 9...h1♛ would have been met by 10.e7+ ♚f7 11.e8♛, mate.
10.♗h4! And again, the h-file is shielded.
10...h1♛ 11.e7+ ♚f7 12.d8♞ Mate. A fantastic finish. Everything fits to a T.

Oleg Pervakov doesn't really need an introduction. His studies are very popular amongst grandmasters, and some people regard him as the greatest study composer of all time. He celebrated his 60th birthday last year. Pervakov is the executive editor of the Russian magazine 64, but everything suggests that he devotes most of his time to endgame studies. Someone recently asked him in Didukh's blog: 'How many hours a day do you spend on average on composing endgame studies?' Pervakov's reply was stunning: 'From the age of 25, I have spent all my life composing studies. If I find a nice idea, I can compose all night. These days I compose with a board or without it, with a computer or without it, in the metro, in the bus, in any place. I may also compose during sex.' That last thing has fortunately never happened to me.

It was hard to make a choice from the rich harvest of Pervakov's crea-

tions. He has composed several complex studies, but I went for a relatively light and extraordinarily well-constructed one.

Oleg Pervakov
1st prize, Persitz Memorial Tourney, Variantim 2019

The position is a bit confusing because of the many hanging pieces. But the rigorous theme in the play soon makes itself felt.

1.♘f7+ Preparing for queening. White could not take the rook: 1.♖xe3? ♕f4+ 2.♔h5 ♕xd6! 3.c8♕ ♕xg6+! 4.♔xg6 stalemate.

1.c8♕? was bad in view of 1...♕f4+, and Black wins.

1...♗xf7 2.c8♕+ ♗g8

3.♖e4! Now the fireworks start. The main purpose of the stunning text-move is to control square f4.

3.♖e5? was insufficient in view of 3...♕f4+ 4.♔g5 ♖e6! 5.♕c3+ ♖f6!, and White will be unable to win.

The queen sacrifice 3.♖f6?, also to establish control of square f4, also fails to lead to victory in view of 3...♖e6! 4.♕c3 ♕h3+ 5.♔g5 ♕g3+ 6.♔f5 ♕h3+ 7.♔f4 ♕h6+ 8.♘g5

Oleg Pervakov, probably the greatest study composer ever, says he may even compose during sex.

♖xf6+ 9.♕xf6+ ♕g7, and Black holds. And again, White could not take the rook in view of stalemate.

3...♖xe4

4.♕f5! A fantastic queen sacrifice, its main point again being control of square f4. 4.♕c3+? was tempting, but narrowly misses the win. After 4...♖d4 5.♕xd4+ ♕xd4 6.♘xd4 Black has the escape 6...♗a2! 7.♘f5 ♔g8! 8.g7 ♔f7, with a draw.

4...♖xg6+! A forced counter-sacrifice by Black to prevent immediate mate.

5.♕xg6! Certainly not 5.♔xg6?, in view of 5...♗h7+. The text also seems to have a drawback.

5...♖e6 6.♘e5! The beautiful thing

about this position is the reciprocal zugzwang. 6.♘h4? was insufficient in view of 6...♗f7!.

6...♖xg6+ 7.♘xg6 Mate.

The 45-year-old Dane Steffen Slumstrup Nielsen is a journalist who, within ten years, has developed into one of the most inventive study composers of our time. He had his debut nine years ago with a first prize in the tournament to mark my 60th birthday, and has added many first prizes to his tally since then. His studies always feature sharp battles full of baiting sacrifices and discovered checks. In the following study we also see both sides sacrificing a queen again.

Steffen Slumstrup Nielsen
Prize, StrateGems 2019

Here, too, we are witnessing an open fight. Both kings are in great danger.

1.♖d4+! White must give check, because 1.♕xb8? ♕e1+! would give Black a draw by perpetual check.

1...♔e2 The only square for the king. After 1...♔e1 2.♖e4+ ♔d1 3.♕xb8 White would quietly win.

2.♖e4+ ♔f3 3.♕g7! A surprising queen sacrifice. Insufficient was 3.♕h7?, since it would leave square a1 unprotected. Black takes over the attack with 3...♕a1+ 4.♘xa1 ♖b1+, and mate.

3...♕c5+! Black also sacrifices his queen. He couldn't take the white queen in view of mate with 4.♘d2.

4.♖d4 It looks feeble, but with this move White can stop the black counterattack.

4...♕f5! Covering square g4. This could not be done with 4...♕h5, which would lead to mate after 5.♘d2+ ♚e2 6.♘f1!, and square h2 has been covered.

5.♘d2+ ♚e3 The alternative 5...♚e2 would fail to 6.♖e4+, and Black would be mated soon.

6.♘f1+ Cornering the black king even more.

6...♕xf1+ The point of the fourth move. The queen sacrifice hands Black the attack.

7.♚xf1 ♖b1+ 8.♚g2 ♗b7+ 9.♚h3 ♖h1+ 10.♚g4 ♗f3+ 11.♚g5 ♖h5+ 12.♚g6 The white king is safe, but Black has another trump: his passed g-pawn.

12...g2 What now?

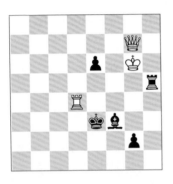

13.♕a7! Creating a deadly discovered check. Insufficient for the win was 13.♚f7? in view of 13...♖d5 14.♖xd5 exd5 15.♕g3 ♚e2, with a theoretically drawn position.

13...♖a5 Black is still not beaten, and the battle rages on. 13...g1♕+ would have failed to 14.♚g4+, of course.

14.♕b6! Not 14.♕xa5?, in view of 14...g1♕+ 15.♚f6 ♗e4! 16.♕c3+ ♚f4, and the black king is safe.

14...♖b5 14...♖a6 15.♖d3+ (15.♕c5 ♖a5 16.♕c3+).

15.♖d3+ 15.♕xb5? g1♕+ 16.♚f6 ♕e1 17.♕c5 (17.♕e5+ ♚f2) 17...♚e2 15.♕a7? ♖a5 16.♕b6 ♖b5.

15...♚xd3 16.♕xb5+ ♚e3 17.♕c5+ Or 17.♕b6+.

17...♚e2 18.♕g1 And wins.

The 50-year-old German Martin Minski was recently made a grandmaster. He is extremely productive, with 613 studies to his name. Like Van der Heijden he must exercise iron discipline, because he is a maths teacher. Maybe he develops ideas while grading tests. Minski likes sacrifices to block files and ranks.

Martin Minski
1st prize, Oleinik Memorial
Tourney 2017

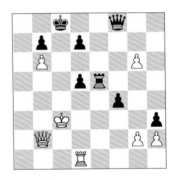

Again a position with exposed kings. It is clear that White must advance his g-pawn.

1.g7! After 1.gxh7? Black would secure perpetual check with 1...♕h4+ 2.♚xe5 ♕e7+. After the text Black does not have this option. White's king can flee to f5, since square f8 is covered by White.

1...♖h4+ Forcing the king forward.

2.♚d5 ♕d1+! Black's best chance. The alternative 2...♘g6 is most easily refuted with 3.♕e2+ ♕xe2 4.♗xe2+ ♚h6 5.♖a7, and wins.

3.♗d3! White could not take the knight. After 3.♚xe5? ♕d4+ his king would have no good squares.

3...♘xd3

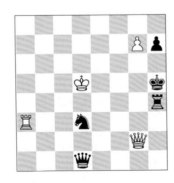

4.♖a5! Covering himself indirectly against a discovered check. Queen-

ing would have yielded him nothing. After 4.g8♕? ♘e5+ 5.♚xe5 ♕d4+ 6.♚e6 ♖e4+ 7.♕xe4 ♕xe4+ Black has a perpetual again.

4...♘e5+! A surprising check: Black opens the d-file and closes the fifth rank. The alternative 4...♘f4+ would lose at once after 5.♚c6+.

5.♚xe5 ♕e1+ It seems as if Black is escaping, but the death blow is imminent.

6.♕e2+! The queen sacrifice distracts the enemy queen. After 6.♚f6+? ♕xa5 7.♕f3+ ♖g4 8.g8♕ ♕a1+ 9.♚e7 ♕a7+ it would be a draw by perpetual check again.

6...♕xe2+ 7.♚f6+ ♚h6 Or 7...♚g4 8.g8♕+.

8.g8♘ Mate. A beautiful finale.

Minski and Nielsen also cooperate fruitfully. The following study is based on the famous game Steinitz-Von Bardeleben, Hastings 1895.

S.S. Nielsen & M. Minski
1st prize, Bukovina-Rumania
unification 100-Anniversary
Tourney 2018

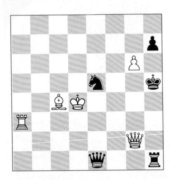

Black is threatening a disruptive check on c5, making the first move forced.

1.♚d2! ♕f6! The only defence. Black covers the rook and threatens a devastating check on e2. But White doesn't care.

2.♖a1! Threatening mate in one. Insufficient was 2.♕a3? in view of 2...♚d8! 3.♖c1 ♕xb6, and Black has defended satisfactorily.

2...♖e2+! Steinitz's rook check with reversed colours. The alternative was

2...♔d8, to prevent the mate, after which White wins with 3.♕b4! d6 4.g7! ♕xg7 5.♕xd6+ ♔e8 6.♕b8+ ♔f7 7.♕xb7+, followed by a queen swap and the b-pawn queening.

3.♔d1! Von Bardeleben had to do the same: move his king along the bottom (top) rank.

3...♖d2+! 4.♔e1! Certainly not 4.♕xd2? ♕xa1+ 5.♕c1+ ♕xc1+ 6.♔xc1 hxg2, and Black wins.

4...♖e2+ 5.♔f1 ♖f2+ 5...hxg2+ 6.♔g1 ♖e1+ was equally insufficient, because then the mate would come from the other side: 7.♖xe1 ♕xb2 8.♖e8 mate.

6.♔g1 ♖xg2+ 7.♔f1

Now the point of White's king moves is revealed: he had to shed his g-pawn to make the queen swap winning.

7...♖f2+ 8.♔e1 ♖e2+ 9.♔d1 ♖d2+ 10.♕xd2! ♕xa1+ 11.♕c1+ ♕xc1+ 12.♔xc1 ♔d8 13.g7 And wins.

There is an obvious difference with the game from 1895: Steinitz's rook sacrifices lead to victory, whereas here they prove to be useless in the end. So it's possible to regard this study as Von Bardeleben's revenge.

The 35-year-old Norwegian Geir Sune Tallaksen Østmoe is not only the youngest of the composers I have mentioned, but also the strongest. With an Elo of 2469, he claims 12th place in the Norwegian rankings. His speciality in the study area is spectacular themes. He managed, for example, to construct a Prokes manoeuvre on both sides. The study will make clear what this means.

Geir Sune Østmoe
1st prize, 6th UAPA Tourney
2018

A natural starting position. Before advancing his f-pawn, White must check the enemy king.

1.♖h1+ ♔g4 2.f7 ♖a8 Here comes the first rook sacrifice:

3.♖d8! ♖xd8 Black is forced to take the rook, since 3...g2 would fail to 4.♖g8+.

4.e7 ♖d4+! The counter-sacrifice, and also the first Prokes manoeuvre. After 4...♗d5+ 5.♔e3 ♖h8 6.e8♕ Black would quietly succumb.

5.♔xd4 ♗xf7 6.♔e3 g2

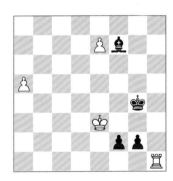

7.♖h4+! The third sacrifice and the second Prokes manoeuvre, this time by White.

7...♔g3 8.♖g4+! The fourth and final rook sacrifice.

8...♔xg4 9.♔xf2 ♔f5 Or 9...♔h3 10.♔g1.

10.a6 ♔e6 11.a7 And wins.

In my book *The Art of the Endgame* I show how the double Prokes manoeuvre – an idea of Tim Krabbé's – can be worked into a study. Østmoe has now added a new element to this. ∎

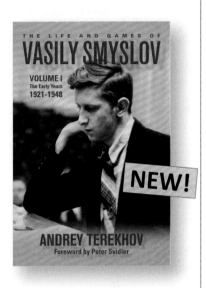

Jennifer Yu

LENNART OOTES

CURRENT ELO: 2328
DATE OF BIRTH: 1 February 2002
PLACE OF BIRTH: Ithaca, NY, USA
PLACE OF RESIDENCE: Ashburn, VA, USA

What was the last great meal you had?
A socially-distanced outdoor picnic with one of my best friends from high school. Pho, bubble tea, and waffles.

What drink brings a smile to your face?
Bubble tea – any kind! It reminds me of hanging out with friends.

Which book would you give to a friend?
Everything I Never Told You, Celeste Ng.

What book is currently on your bedside table?
A Brief History of Time, Stephen Hawking.

What is your all-time favourite movie?
Perks of Being A Wallflower.

And your favourite TV series?
Bones, The Office, Friends, Arrow.

Do you have a favourite actor?
I can't go wrong with Leo DiCaprio.

And a favourite actress?
Anya Taylor-Joy. *The Queen's Gambit* was amazing.

What music are you listening to?
Kanye West, Awesome Mix (Guardians of the Galaxy Soundtrack), Joji.

Is there a painting that moves you?
The Persistence of Memory, Salvador Dali.

What is your earliest chess memory?
I learned how to play chess in a chess club at my elementary school. For some reason, the club only existed for one month before getting cancelled. We would get chess-piece keychains as prizes and I wanted to collect all of the pieces. Sadly, I never did.

Who is your favourite chess player of all time?
I never had a favourite player. I always looked at a variety of players' games. However, I'm following a lot of live events now and plan on studying the classics, so that may change soon!

Is there a chess book that had a profound influence on you?
Susan Polgar: *Chess Tactics for Champions*. The first tactics book that I worked on by myself while waiting for my mom to pick me up from after-school programs.

What was your best result ever?
Winning the 2019 US Women's Chess Championship with 10/11.

And the best game you played?
Zatonskih-Yu, 2019 US Women's Chess Championship. This game won me the Championship with a round to spare.

What was the most exciting chess game you ever saw?
Very recent, Dubov-Karjakin, Russian Super Final 2020.

What is your favourite square?
c4!! As it represents the English Opening.

Do you have any superstitions concerning chess?
I used to have a lucky necklace, but then I got tired of it and now I just play chess.

Facebook, Instagram, Snapchat, or?
Instagram. I mainly use social media to keep up with friends.

What is your life motto?
Just wing it (unfortunately this doesn't work as well for openings).

When were you happiest?
In the winter of 2019, after I got accepted to my dream college. I could relax in school and spend more time with friends. Unfortunately I didn't get a second semester of senior year because of Covid.

Who or what would you like to be if you weren't yourself?
A penguin.

Which three people would you like to invite for dinner?
Genghis Khan, Alexander Alekhine, Taylor Swift.

What is the best piece of advice you were ever given?
For chess: play each game move by move.

Is there something you'd love to learn?
I'm currently learning to read and write in Chinese. I'd love to learn other languages like Russian and German.

What would people be surprised to know about you?
I don't like lettuce in sandwiches (with the exception of hamburgers).

What is your greatest fear?
Being forgotten and losing the people I love (deep).

If you could change one thing in the chess world, what would it be?
More female chess players.

Is a knowledge of chess useful in everyday life?
Sadly, I haven't yet found out how to use Slav theory in everyday life. But you can learn good life lessons from chess.